SCOTT JACKSON

PreMeditated SUCCESS
IN LIFE

The Power of Personal Vision

Morgan James Publishing • New York

TESTIMONIALS

"PreMeditated Success is a must read that offers the lessons of business and life to lead and succeed. Follow Scott's advice and you will get ahead in a fast paced world where the only rule is personal responsibility."

-Myers Barnes
Master Sales Trainer
Author of Closing Strong and Reach the Top on New Home Sales

"This is an amazing book, beautifully written by someone who is living proof of premeditated success. Scott shares important material that is unique, adds massive value and provides the tools and strategies to make significant changes in the reader's life – all the ingredients of a best seller!"

-Ann McIndoo
Author's Coach
Palm Springs, California

"PreMeditated Success in Life is a no-nonsense, user-friendly guide to putting the Law of Attraction into Action. This is solid work!"

-Mark Moffitt
Producer of the hit movie Beyond the Secret and the television series Life Coach

"PreMeditated Success in Life reflects Scott's deep understanding of the laws that govern the way we think and behave. If you are serious about improving your results and the overall quality of your life, this powerful lesson in life leadership is a must read."

-Paul Martinelli
President, LifeSuccess Consultants

PreMeditated
SUCCESS
IN LIFE

by Scott Jackson © 2009 all rights reserved.

Library of Congress Control Number: 2008939553
ISBN: 978-1-60037-518-7   (Paperback)
ISBN: 978-1-60037-519-4   (Hardcover)

Published by:
Morgan James Publishing, LLC
1225 Franklin Avenue Suite 325
Garden City, NY 11530-1693

Toll Free 800-485-4943
www.MorganJamesPublishing.com

Cover & Interior Design by:
3 Dog Design
www.3dogdesign.net

General Editor:
Heather Campbell

CONTENTS

DEDICATION

To Bill Kaufman, my mentor and friend; rest peacefully.

ACKNOWLEDGEMENTS

I wish to thank Joyce, David, and Will for their endless patience and support of all my crazy adventures—at home with the three of you is as good as it gets; the "A-Team," which includes Jason Bradley, Jeannette Burt, Lee Anne Rose, J.D. MacNair, Jessica Winfree, Monica Riga, and Beth Hall—without your hard work and loyal support, this project and many others would have never gotten off the ground; my mom, who loves everything I have ever done; my friend and mentor Grant Hollett; results coach Brenda Schenke; author's coach Ann McIndoo; business partners Scott Bame and Tim Henson; and the entire teams of Southern Coast Vacations, Southern Coast Builders, and Weichert Realtors Southern Coast.

INTRODUCTION

One of the greatest sources of frustration for people is the false belief that self-discipline is the key to success. While it appears that self-discipline can result in success, in reality, the people who lead remarkably successful lives do so by pursuing what they love and value most. It's having amazing clarity as to what they want out of life that fuels their efforts and makes their success unavoidable, not self-discipline.

PreMeditated Success is a powerful tool for clarifying your personal values and vision, as well as for initiating predictable cycles of success. As you break free of self-imposed constraints, you will become a powerful influence in the lives of those around you. Whether you are seeking wealth, fitness, healthy relationships, or meaningful contribution, this innovative approach to true fulfillment and life leadership guarantees you the purest form of success—the pleasurable pursuit of what you love and value most!

PreMeditated
-adjective
done deliberately; planned in advance[1]

Success
-noun
1. the favorable or prosperous results of attempts or endeavors
2. the attainment of wealth, position, honors, or the like
3. a successful performance or achievement[2]

CHAPTER

1

Treasure Hunting 101

On July 20, 1985, Mel Fisher and his team of treasure hunters successfully completed their sixteen-year search for the *Nuestra Señora de Atocha*, a Spanish galleon that sank in a hurricane near Key West in September 1622. Known as the world's greatest treasure hunter, Fisher located over forty tons of silver and gold valued in excess of $450 million.

The search was not always easy. Fisher's life was not immune to the tragedies and heartbreaks that occur over any sixteen-year span of living. In spite of great personal loss and sacrifice, Fisher never lost faith in his quest; he *knew* he would find his treasure. "Today's the day!" he insisted. "Today's the day!" … for sixteen years!

Even as a child, Fisher dreamed of the sea. With homemade diving gear, he began exploring lakes near his home in Indiana at the age of eleven. After serving in World War II and a brief career as a chicken rancher, Fisher opened one of the first scuba shops in the world in

1953. He loved diving and was constantly inventing gear for himself and other divers.

Shortly after meeting treasure hunter Kip Wagner while on a diving trip in Florida in 1964, Fisher made his first major find: thousands of gold coins carpeting the ocean floor. His life as a treasure hunter had begun. If Fisher couldn't find the equipment he needed, he invented it. Much of the equipment he invented in his earliest searches would later lead him to the *Atocha*.

The search for the *Atocha* began in 1969. After two years, Fisher and his crew discovered a few silver coins. Two years later, he recovered three silver bars from the seabed and, after another two years, a bronze cannon bearing the name *Atocha*. By 1975, six years into the search, plenty of clues told them that they were on the right track, but there had also been enough fruitless searches to send most men home, either discouraged by their failure to find the mother lode or satisfied with what they had found. Though many men before him had sought the great treasures that the Atocha offered without success, Fisher knew it was his to find. His great enthusiasm and commitment enabled him to maintain investors through times of seemingly little success.

Five years later, in 1980, Fisher's team located a portion of the Atocha's sister ship, the *Margarita*, along with a fortune in gold bars, silver coins, and jewelry. And finally, in 1985, after sixteen years of searching and never giving up, Kane Fisher, Mel's son, informed his father that the long search was over; the *Atocha* had been found.

Can you imagine what it would be like to ask an investor to back you while you look for sunken treasure? Can you imagine investing in someone whose business plan consisted of searching for lost treasure? Though the idea of gaining financial support for such an adventure might have seemed far-fetched to most people, Fisher's unwavering conviction, his absolute certainty that the treasure was theirs to find, enabled his team to continue its quest long after other treasure hunters had run out of money and enthusiasm.

Of all the people on the planet Earth who dreamed of finding the *Atocha*, how is it that Mel Fisher was the one to succeed? Many people knew that the *Atocha* was "out there," as it had been for hundreds of years, yet only a few actually looked for it. And of those who did, most gave up after a few attempts. How is it that Fisher was able to succeed where so many others had failed? Was it research? Advances in technology? Fisher's incredible spirit? I'm sure these and many other factors played a considerable role in his success, but without question, the primary reason Fisher found the Atocha is that, more than anyone else in the world, *he was the one looking for it!* When you think about it, the odds that Fisher would be the one to find the *Atocha* were actually pretty good.

The fact that a sixteen-year search yielded results is not surprising. The fact that Fisher enthusiastically continued his search for sixteen years is beyond what most of us can imagine. What I find most impressive about Fisher's life is not the fact the he found the treasure but that he was able to spend his life as a treasure hunter year after year on the crystal clear water of the Caribbean, *knowing* that "Today's the day." Imagine the excitement and anticipation of knowing that today is the day you will find your treasure! Today's the day your long search, your hard work, your dedication, and your commitment will pay off. Today's the day you reunite with old friends, repair broken relationships, and create lasting change in your life. How can you not approach life with enthusiasm and joy when you know that today's the day?

It might appear to the layperson that Fisher's success was simply an extreme example of self-discipline paying off. Fortunately, this is not true. I say fortunately because most of us have learned through experience that if our success in life is contingent solely upon self-discipline, we are in big trouble. When it comes to creating lasting change in our lives, self-discipline has repeatedly let us down. Although many aspects of the search required a disciplined approach, the search itself was a labor of love. Fisher loved being a treasure hunter. He loved diving; he loved the water; he loved his life. The fact is that without that passion, that certainty that we are on the right track, self-discipline is unsustainable. Without the support of an underlying belief system to fuel our efforts, we quickly give up.

In the following chapters we will examine the relationship between our thoughts and our actions. A deep understanding of how one drives the other is essential to creating a successful life. Some teach that attitude is everything, others that it is simply our actions that make the difference. Both are right. Both are wrong. Had Mel Fisher just sat on his couch proclaiming "Today's the day" without taking action, his great attitude would have had little value. Had he attempted to find the *Atocha* relying only on discipline, without the sense of certainty that he was pursuing his life's mission, he surely would have given up long before the sixteen-year effort paid off.

CHAPTER

2

Among the Gifted

Without question, Mel Fisher was gifted. His natural good spirit and optimism, combined with the creativity to overcome any obstacle, were with him from birth. The imagination necessary to invent what did not exist was, in my opinion, God given. Just as you have always suspected, all of the remarkably successful people in history were gifted. Is Tiger Woods gifted? Eric Clapton? Anthony Robbins? Donald Trump? Was Mother Teresa gifted? Ben Franklin? Dale Carnegie? The answer to all of the above is yes, absolutely yes! In order to live a remarkably successful life, you do indeed have to be gifted. Fortunately, *we are all gifted!*

The difference between those perceived as gifted and the rest of the population is that the ones perceived as gifted have opened their gifts. They do not necessarily have more gifts than the average person, but they certainly seem to get the most enjoyment from the ones they have.

In the booklet you[2], Price Pritchett points out that the special skills and unique talents that you have exhibited over the years are the gifts you opened and enjoyed. How many more gifts are waiting? Pritchett makes the case that for every gift you open, hundreds more are waiting to be unwrapped and taken out of the package. Everything you need is already available to you. This is a common theme among all of the great teachers of success I have studied.

How do we find these unopened gifts? We pursue our passions. Passion always surrounds our gifts. Think about it. Isn't it true that we are best at the very things we most enjoy doing? When it comes to things we are passionate about, we have plenty of energy. We do not need to be disciplined to pursue that which brings us pleasure. If you are really good at something but you don't enjoy doing it, then that is not one of your gifts. It is just the result of learning how to do something well through discipline, and rarely will this lead to a remarkable level of success.

I will often begin a workshop by asking the simple question, "How many of you would like to live a successful life?" Without exception, everyone raises his or her hand. I follow up with, "How will you know when you get there?" Usually they look at me as if I have asked the dumbest question ever, but few can come up with an answer without really thinking about it. How about you? The fact that you are reading this book is an indication that you have a greater-than-average desire to enjoy success. But what exactly does success mean to you? What has to happen in order for your life to be successful? Take a few minutes to complete the vision statements that follow. Live out of your imagination and describe your successful life. Don't get hung up on getting the wording just right or what order you should list things; just pick up your pen and start writing. Don't stop until you have at least ten ways to enjoy success. From this point on, we will be referring to this as your **Personal Vision of Success.**

EXAMPLE: I enjoy great success in life now that...
- My company is ranked number one in market share
- I am a lean 180 pounds
- My book is a national best seller

Be sure to complete the statement at the bottom of the page before moving on to Chapter 3.

Personal Vision of Success

I enjoy great success in life now that...

- _____
- _____
- _____
- _____
- _____
- _____
- _____
- _____
- _____
- _____

The reason(s) I have not been successful up to now is(are)...

_____

_____

CHAPTER

3

Navigational Aids

S top! If you didn't complete the statements at the end of Chapter 2, please go back and do it now. Write it down. There is great power in putting pen to paper. Throughout this book I have provided space for you to write down answers to specific questions and capture your ideas. In the process, you will create the tools needed to build a successful life. If you truly want to create lasting change in your life, complete every assignment before moving on. Reading this book without "filling in the blanks" might inspire you for a brief period of time, but it will not help you create the lasting change you desire.

One of my great passions in life is sailing. I love everything about it. Sailing slows me down and fills me with a sense of freedom. It may appear that sailors are just being pushed along by the breeze, but there is a definite science to sailing; we are governed by the laws of nature. If you work with the elements, you can go anywhere there is water regardless of wind direction; work against the elements, and you find yourself trapped in irons and unable to move in any direction. As a blue water sailor, one of the most important skills you must learn is how to navigate. In order to navigate, you must first know where you are, and you must be decisive as to where you want to go. You will need up-to-date charts, a reliable compass, and navigational aids such as buoys and lighthouses. Without these tools, you are lost and at the mercy of the elements surrounding you. With these tools, you can stay on course in the stormiest conditions and through the most treacherous waters. Navigating through life successfully is no different. We must have up-to-date charts (our paradigm), a reliable compass (our values and principles), and aids to navigation (our support systems and vision). But most important, we need to know two things: where we are and where we want to go.

With this in mind, I would like for you to refer back to your Personal Vision of Success that you completed at the end of Chapter 2. Are you developing a sense of where you want to go? You always have the option of choosing new destinations in the future, but for now, do you have an outcome in mind?

I once asked a class of new real estate agents how much money they were going to earn in their very first year. As the agents answered, I wrote their income goals on the board for everyone to see. The answers ranged from $30,000 to $100,000, with one exception: an attractive woman who appeared to be in her early fifties confidently stated that $750,000 would be a good number for her. I wrote it on the board, and unlike the rest of those in the room, I didn't flinch.

I went around the room again, this time asking what made the students pick the specific income goals they chose. Some just wanted to make as much money as they were making at their last job; some stated that they needed to make their goals just to pay their bills;

and others viewed a six-figure income as the top of the heap. Some hadn't really thought about it and just tossed out a number in the middle that wouldn't draw attention to them. At last I made it to the woman with the goal of $750,000. She said she knew that the very top agents earned well over a million dollars a year, but because she was brand new to the business, she scaled it back to $750,000. There were a few snickers in the room. I asked her to tell us a little about her background. She was about ten years older than I had guessed; she had retired a self-made millionaire when she was in her late forties. Not only was she ready to get back in the game, she intended to make a lot of money while playing it. The others stopped snickering at this point.

I circled the $30,000 goal and the $750,000 goal and asked, "Based on nothing more than their stated goals, who do you think is going to make the most money this year?" It was unanimous. Everyone was sure that the person with the highest expectations would achieve the most. We know this intuitively, yet we still tend to limit our thinking. We play it safe. We use our past to predict our future. "Who is better off," I pressed, "the agent that exceeds her goal of $30,000 by 20 percent or the agent that comes up short of her $750,000 goal by 20 percent?"

Exceptional people are not the product of average thinking!

Please read through your Personal Vision of Success again, and as you do, *think about the way you think*. Are you using your current situation as the standard by which you measure success? Are you allowing past failures to temper your expectations for the future? Is fear of failure causing you to set the bar so low that even if you clear the bar you won't win? For now, just ponder how you ponder.

Now let's look at how you completed the statement below:

The reason(s) I have not been successful up to now is(are)...

Are other people holding you back? Have you been so badly wronged in the past that it is stopping you from moving forward now? Is it your environment? Are you a current or past victim of abuse? Is "the man" keeping you down? Is it your race? Gender? How you were raised? Do you lack education? Do you come from a broken home? Are you physically unattractive? Are you obese? Did your mother make you eat everything on your plate? Maybe you never knew your mother. Were your parents alcoholics? Were you picked on as a child? Is your zodiac sign an obstacle? Did you break a mirror, walk under a ladder, or see a black cat cross your path? Was it the quality of the public schools? Did your college of choice reject you? Was it your first wife? Your second husband? Did your team lose the big game? Did you get cut from the team? Is your boss a jerk? Are your employees idiots? Was your heart broken? If the federal government had just... If the real estate market hadn't crashed... If the stock market would have gone the way I expected... Do you just have plain old-fashioned bad luck? I could fill this book with reasons that people give for not succeeding. Some of these you may relate to strongly; others are laughable.

Thank God none of this is true! I am not saying that what you wrote down is not true; your boss may very well be a jerk. What I am saying is that the idea that you cannot succeed because of it is not true. I don't care what you put down as your reason(s) for not succeeding to this point; whatever it may be, I promise you that if you will look, you find someone with the same circumstances, or worse, who has overcome them to lead a remarkably successful life. This is a fact, and I challenge anyone to prove me wrong. It is my intention for millions of people to read and use this book, and that means millions of reasons, none of them true. Sometimes when people have a large portion of their lives invested around a shortcoming (their own or someone else's) or a situation they see as beyond their control, they get angry when someone suggests that their reasoning is not too sound. I understand how they feel. I had to swallow a few bitter pills myself along the way. All I can say is, like it or not, it is the truth. Do you want proof? Complete the following statement and then decide whether it is true or false:

The reason(s) I have not been successful up to now is(are) (insert your very best reason here) _____

_____

_____ ,

and throughout the history of man, without exception, no one has ever overcome this and gone on to lead a remarkably successful life! True or False?

Human beings are amazing. We can overcome anything. What an inspirational life Christopher Reeve led *after* becoming a quadriplegic; Lance Armstrong overcame testicular cancer to win a record seven consecutive Tour de France races; Nelson Mandela became president of South Africa after decades of wrongful imprisonment. No matter what comes our way, we are free to choose our response. That is what responsibility means—the freedom to respond. We surrender that freedom whenever we look outside ourselves to apportion blame for our circumstances. I realize that this can be a difficult concept to grasp, especially if we are in the habit of absolving ourselves of responsibility for our lack of success.

We are navigating rocky waters here. Remember the two pieces of information you must have for navigation? *Where are you right now?* Are you willing to assume 100 percent responsibility for your success? *Where do you want to go?* Are you getting clear as to just what your successful life will look like? The rest of this book is about creating the tools you need to reach your destiny. Today's the day! The truth will indeed set you free.

"So oftentimes it happens
That we live our lives in chains
And we never even know we have the key..."

Already Gone - The Eagles 3
Written by Robert Arnold Strandlund and Jack Tempchin

CHAPTER

4

Creative Thinking

When I was sixteen years old, my family went flat broke. We lost the house I grew up in to foreclosure, and just prior to my sophomore year in high school we moved to a new town to start over. My mother, as the only employed member of the family, stayed behind until my father, my brother, or I could find work. Had any of us imagined that would take over nine months, we probably would have come up with a better plan.

It was a long, cold winter. I discovered what it was like to be miss-a-meal poor, and I didn't much care for it. Though my brush with being broke was relatively brief, its effect on me was long-lasting. Shortly before my seventeenth birthday, I landed a job washing dishes at a new restaurant, and not long afterward, I dropped out of school. I admit now that that wasn't the smartest decision I ever made, but at the time it made perfect sense; after all, I wasn't going to college and several of my classmates had already quit. Like my classmates, I valued having a job, however menial it may have been, far more than I valued a high school diploma.

Although I started down the same path as my fellow dropouts, it is interesting to note how different we became over the years. While my friends seemed bound by decisions made as teenagers, I became free to pursue my dreams. I had no advantages over my peers, at least not the kind most people recognize. I wasn't smarter, richer, or better looking; I didn't have friends in high places; and I didn't have any unusual talents that I could cash in on.

What enabled me to go from high school dropout dishwasher to millionaire? The short answer is that *my thinking evolved*. The same mind that thought it would be a good idea to drop out of school evolved into a reliable source of creative intelligence.

I spent the next twenty years of my life working for the company that hired me to wash dishes. I am pretty sure they didn't plan on my hanging around that long; after all, they were just looking for a dishwasher. For some reason the restaurant owner, Lattie Upchurch, saw potential in me far beyond what I saw in myself, and over the years his presence in my life became a powerful influence on the way I thought. When you start out as a dishwasher, there is plenty of room to move up, and as the business expanded to include multiple locations, I was able to grow along with it. Though the time came that I had to leave the company to continue my growth, I will always be grateful to Mr. Upchurch for holding me to a higher standard.

The fact that how we think is influenced by those around us is undeniable. I have heard it said that if you really want to know what you are like, just look at your friends—you are just like them. Looking back, I know that if I hadn't moved, I would never have dropped out of school. I say this with conviction. The idea of dropping out of school would have been absolutely unacceptable among the friends I grew up with. No matter how badly I wanted or needed to work,

I never would have even *thought* about dropping out of school. It wasn't until after I moved away and some of my newfound friends quit school that I began to entertain the idea. The more I thought about quitting school, the better I liked the idea; after all, there was no money to pay for college, right? By the time I actually got around to dropping out, I had very sound reasons in my own mind that I was doing the right thing; in fact, it seemed like my only option. In just over one year, the idea of dropping out of school went from unacceptable, to acceptable, to actionable. It is frightening just how quickly and completely my thinking changed.

It has been my experience that most people are very careless when it comes to where they seek validation. Often they will accept the opinions and advice of people in worse shape than themselves. I have seen people invest tens of thousands of dollars based on the advice they received from someone who could barely pay his bills. In 2000, 85 percent of global assets were owned by only 10 percent of the population, while the bottom 50 percent of the population combined owned barely 1 percent.[3] The overwhelming majority of the people you meet—nearly everyone, in fact—can provide only really bad advice when it comes to money. But somehow their numbers alone give us comfort. After all, everyone agrees! Everyone is buying, so I should buy! Everyone is selling, so I should sell! Just the fact that everyone agrees with you should be cause for alarm. The masses may often lead you astray.

Rich people tend to hang out with other rich people not because they are snobs but because the rich know that becoming wealthy is mostly about how you think, and how you think can be greatly influenced by those around you. When teachers gather socially, the talk is about education; when Realtors gather socially, the talk is about real estate. People who are struggling financially speak of hard times; when rich people gather, the talk is of wealth and abundance. The way people talk is the way people think; it is impossible to speak and hear about being poor, fat, or unhappy without thinking about being poor, fat, and unhappy.

In July 2007, *The New England Journal of Medicine* published a study that followed more than twelve thousand people for thirty-two years. The report was centered on the effects of social networks on individuals, and the researchers concluded that by simply having an obese friend, a person increased the likelihood that he or she would become obese as well by 57 percent! Obesity is contagious! So are poverty, a bad attitude, and anything else you can think about. You should be very selective about with whom you spend time.

People rarely rise above the expectations of their peers. When we see those around us gaining weight, it becomes acceptable for us to gain weight; when our associates struggle financially, it becomes the norm; and if our buddies are dropping out of school, why not us? It is not maliciousness on the part of our peers that causes this; it is just that most people share a very low standard for success. It isn't that the population at large isn't capable of great things; it's that the people in it just don't see themselves as capable of greatness. We tend to look around us to determine what is possible. My new friends certainly were not at fault for not challenging my decision to quit school. My actions fit well within their paradigm, or model of acceptable behavior. I lived up to the expectations of my peers.

Does this mean you have to dump your friends? No, just be aware of the pitfalls. I didn't run off my old friends, but I did fill up my life with new friends. I am extremely picky when it comes to whom I allow to influence me. I still have some old friends who suffer from bad attitudes, and I limit the amount of time I spend with them.

Do you see the irony in reading a book written by a high school dropout warning you about to whom you should pay attention? I love America! Let's take a look at what some really smart people have written about thinking:

"All that we are is the result of what we have thought. The mind is everything. What we think we become."

Hindu Prince Gautama Siddharta, the founder of Buddhism

"As a man thinks in his heart, so is he."

Proverbs 23:7

"It is what a man thinks of himself that really determines his fate."

Henry David Thoreau

It isn't what you have, or who you are, or where you are, or what you are doing that makes you happy or unhappy. It is what you think about."

Dale Carnegie

"A man is what he thinks about all day long."
Ralph Waldo Emerson

Does this mean that any stray thought that pops into our heads can lead us to ruin? My answer is no, although the potential is there. The muck we get stuck in isn't the result of a passing thought; it is the product of *chronic stinking thinking.* It doesn't happen overnight. A bad idea or negative thought enters our minds, and instead of immediately recoiling from it as if it were a poisonous snake (which it is), we give it safe haven. We nurture it and allow it to take root. Anger, resentments, prejudices, and fear exacerbate our chronic stinking thinking to the point that our right way of thinking is lost. The areas of your life that cause you the most pain are almost always tied to chronic stinking thinking, and self-discipline will be of little help as long as this condition persists.

Wherever you are right now, stop for just a minute and look around. Everything you see that is created by man, and I mean everything, began as a thought. You will find no exceptions. Success in any area of your life will be of your own creation, and all creations begin with thoughts. There is no other way.

You are responsible for the way you think. It is not the responsibility of your peers, your boss, your spouse, or anyone else. Now go back and think of the first rule of navigation, *knowing where you are.* Then begin to think of knowing where you are in terms of *knowing that you are responsible.* No matter what comes your way, you have the power to choose how you will respond, even how you will *think.* If you are unwilling to assume this responsibility, this book will be of little use to you, for this is the foundation on which we are building with tools that will enable you to shape your thinking; it is your thinking that shapes your life. Without knowing where you are, *that you are responsible*, you will be unable to get to where you want to go and to achieve your Personal Vision of Success.

CHAPTER

5

The Discipline Myth

I n 1940, Albert E. N. Gray presented at the National Association of Underwriters annual convention a speech that is now commonly known as "The Common Denominator of Success." Gray, a nationally known speaker, writer, and trainer for the insurance industry came to the following conclusion: "The common denominator of success—the secret of success of every man who has ever been successful—lies in the fact that he formed the habit of doing things that failures don't like to do."

Gray came to this conclusion in an effort to explain why some life insurance agents would enter the business and prosper while other agents with similar backgrounds and levels of education would enter the business and fail. While I do not doubt the facts behind his statement—obviously successful agents are doings some things that the failures are not—I do question the accuracy of his conclusion. I believe he found a common denominator of success, not *the* common denominator of success.

Gray's model of success looks like this:

ACTION

↓

RESULTS

↓

REPEAT

Although Gray doesn't offer any details, he states that at some point you will need a strong sense of purpose in order to continue doing the things you don't like to do, which suggests to me that he knew his model was incomplete.

The Discipline Myth

Most of us have been taught that success is a matter of discipline; certainly that is the underlying message of Gray's presentation. You're not doing well in school? Be disciplined. Are you overweight? Be disciplined! If you want to be great at piano, you had better be disciplined. You need to make more sales? Just be disciplined. You don't have to like it; you just have to do it! Just exactly what does it mean to employ self-discipline? Let's look at how discipline is defined by Dictionary.com:

Discipline: *—noun*
1 training to act in accordance with rules; drill.

2 activity, exercise, or a regimen that develops or improves a skill; training.

3 punishment inflicted by way of correction and training.

4 the rigor or training effect of experience, adversity, etc.

5 behavior in accord with rules of conduct; behavior and order maintained by training and control.

6 a set or system of rules and regulations.

7 *Ecclesiastical.* the system of government regulating the practice of a church as distinguished from its doctrine.

8 an instrument of punishment, esp. a whip or scourge, used in the practice of self-mortification or as an instrument of chastisement in certain religious communities.

9 a branch of instruction or learning.

Only two definitions here (2 and 3) fit the way we commonly refer to self-discipline. What does self-discipline feel like? That all depends on which definition of *discipline* you are using. If you are passionate about what you are doing, you are using the definition *"activity, exercise, or a regimen that develops or improves a skill,"* and the work involved will be pleasurable.

If, on the other hand, you are making yourself do things you really don't like to do, self-discipline will feel very much like "punishment inflicted by way of correction and training."

I don't know about you, but doing the things I don't like to do for long periods of time feels like punishment to me. If you have chastised yourself in the past for your lack of self-discipline, I suggest you change the phrase to *self-punishment* and see if you still wish you had more of it!

I know it appears that the truly gifted are the product of rigorous self-discipline. After all, we hear of the hours upon hours that they spend out of the spotlight with no one looking over their shoulders, doing the things that improve their skills and enhance their God-given talents. Discipline defined as an "activity, exercise, or a regimen that develops or improves a skill" plays a major role and occurs naturally in the development of their gifts. We assume that because we don't like doing those things, they don't like doing those things either. Because it would be punishment for you, you assume that it is punishment for them as well.

I hate yard work. You could not pay me to cut my own grass if I could find any other option. If you ever see me working in my yard, you know that I am displaying tremendous self-discipline— the self-punishment kind. My friend Vicki, on the other hand, loves working in her yard. I'm not sure that there are many things in life that bring her more pleasure. The discipline she calls upon is far different from the discipline I use when it comes to yard work. It is not punishment for her; it is the pursuit of passion. The type of discipline that is tied to our gifts feels completely different than the discipline required to continue doing something we don't like to do. I will never be a great gardener unless my attitude toward gardening undergoes a transformation or paradigm shift. I am more than capable of doing the gardening "stuff" that Vicki likes to do, but I don't like doing it. I know from past experience that the day will come when I will forget to adjust the sprinklers, I won't feel like cutting the grass, and I will choose sailing over pulling weeds. I might start out doing everything I am supposed to do, but I will be unable to sustain the effort over any substantial period of time.

Consider the remarkably successful, gifted people we mentioned in Chapter 2:

Tiger Woods had won sixty Professional Golfers' Association (PGA) events, including thirteen majors, as of September 2007.

Eric Clapton, rock guitarist and singer, has performed and recorded with the Yardbirds, John Mayall's Bluesbreakers, Cream, Blind Faith, and Derek and the Dominoes. In addition to having a prolific solo career, he has played and recorded with most of the great names of rock music.

Author, speaker, and success coach **Anthony (Tony) Robbins** has coached world leaders, including George H. W. Bush, Bill Clinton, Mikhail Gorbachev, Princess Diana, Dwayne Johnson (better known as the Rock), and Andre Agassi.

Donald Trump is a real estate developer, mogul, and star of the hit NBC reality series *The Apprentice.*

Mother Teresa, winner of the 1979 Nobel Peace Prize, was beatified by Pope John Paul II in 2003.

Considered the "wisest American," diplomat and statesman **Ben Franklin** was also a philosopher, publisher, inventor, and scientist. His sayings in Poor Richard's Almanac are still quoted today. His other contributions include being America's first postmaster general as well as founding the American Philosophical Society, which later became the University of Pennsylvania.

American lecturer and writer on self-improvement **Dale Carnegie** wrote *How to Win Friends and Influence People* (1936), a runaway best seller.

In your opinion, is their level of success the result of naturally occurring discipline that appears as the result of pursuing one's passion or the product of a white-knuckled, just-do-it brand of self-discipline?

I am not saying that we should go through life and never do anything that we don't want to do. To be a good friend, husband, father, neighbor, boss, co-worker, teammate, crew member, group member, bandmate, or citizen, we must be passionate in our willingness to help others and serve the greater good, even when we don't feel like it. My point is that you will never find your gifts or rise to greatness if you focus your efforts on doing things you really don't like to do.

CHAPTER

6

PreMeditated Model of Success

Have you ever heard the old saying "One man's heaven is another man's hell?" Whether something is good or bad, whether it brings us pleasure or pain, is determined by our paradigms, our view or perspective of that specific event or situation. In short, it is about how we *think*; it is the meaning we attach to a situation or event that determines us. To better explain this, we must build a more complete model of success.

Everything begins with a thought or idea. This is the first block of the PreMeditated Model of Success.

It is not my lack of ability to do gardening chores that does not bode well for my front yard, it is the way I think about gardening. How could my thinking be so different from that of my friend with the green thumb?

Have you ever been involved in debates or arguments with people and you just couldn't figure out how they could be so off-base in their conclusions? And the more you tried to make them see the obvious, the angrier they became? Were they taking the very same data you used in support of your argument and misinterpreting it in a way that supported theirs? Did you sense that they were as frustrated with you as you were with them? Were you so sure that you were right that to *even consider otherwise* felt like blasphemy? Behold the power of paradigms!

A good definition of *paradigm* as it relates to this discussion is "a set of assumptions, concepts, values, and practices that constitutes a way of viewing reality." A paradigm governs how we think. It is our own personal rulebook for the way things really are. There are many factors—including genetic predisposition, the environments in which we were raised, and our social networks—that have played major roles in shaping our paradigms. The way we think is always in alignment with our paradigm. In the coming chapters, we will look at ways to change our paradigms, to initiate a paradigm shift, if you choose to, but for now just know that your paradigm, to a great extent, is the way you think. From our thoughts, we form our beliefs and attitudes.

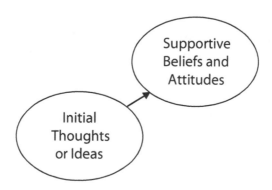

Our beliefs and attitudes must fit within our paradigm; it cannot be otherwise. Just as an apple seed cannot produce a grapefruit, thinking negatively about a situation cannot produce a positive attitude. If my paradigm initiates the thought that high school dropouts cannot become wealthy, it would be impossible for me to believe otherwise without a shift in my thinking.

From our attitudes and beliefs, we form realistic expectations.

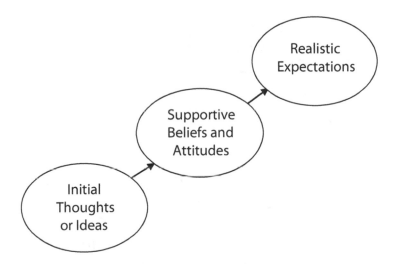

Expectations have to be realistic based upon our beliefs and attitudes. What is a realistic income goal for a high school dropout? The answer will fit my paradigm. Does my thinking allow for a six-figure income? From here, it is a simple matter of taking the appropriate actions to realize my expectations.

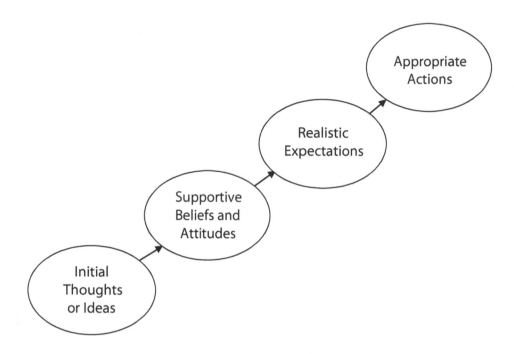

What do I mean by *appropriate actions*? If I was working within a paradigm that limited my beliefs and expectations to the point that I believed that a high school dropout could never rise above the level of a laborer, even the act of applying for a management position would be inappropriate; that action would not fit my paradigm. Actions lead to predictable results.

We don't get what we want in life; we get what we expect. Because I never applied for the job or expressed an interest in management, I never got the job. The results were just as I predicted when I first thought about it: "See? I told you they would never make me manager!"

The PreMeditated Model of Success

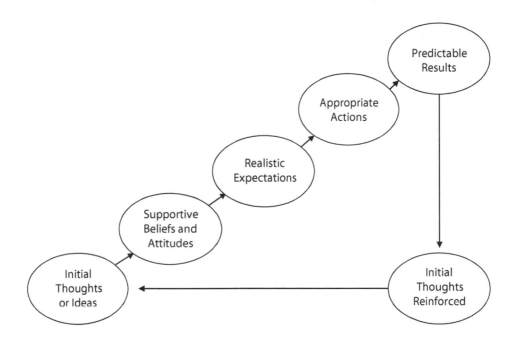

This model works equally well whether you are going up or down. Let's look at this model using two different paradigms for fitness and exercise. The two examples I am using here are people I know personally. The first example is Ted, a fifty-three-year-old real estate agent who attended a series of workshops I was facilitating on creating lasting change. The workshop was held in early January, and I began by asking if anyone had made a New Year's resolution that he or she was already struggling with or had given up on altogether. Ted informed us that he had promised himself that he would begin exercising, but after a few half-hearted attempts, he had quit. I asked Ted what he thought about exercising in general, and he offered the following;

- It's hard!
- I don't like it.
- I don't have time.
- I have to make myself do it.
- It makes me tired.
- I can get in shape later.
- It's not fun.
- It's painful.
- I always quit.

Ted's Paradigm

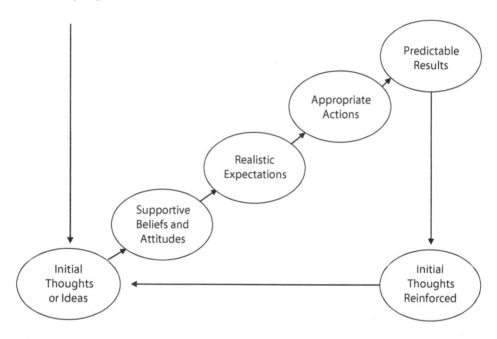

Obviously, Ted's attitudes and beliefs associated with exercise were not very positive. He expected it to be hard, painful, and unsustainable. With that mindset, why not quit sooner rather than later? The results were as predicted; by January 8, Ted had given up. Eight months later, Ted suffered a major heart attack. Self-discipline had failed completely.

My next example, Ximena White, was born in Santiago, Chile. She came to America on a golf scholarship in 1974. The first time I saw her, she was doing chin-ups at a local gym. I have no idea how many reps she did that morning, but she had the attention of everyone in the room. On her last rep, she stopped halfway down, with elbows bent at 90 degrees, and hung there for what seemed like an eternity. The greatest impression she made on me that morning was not the astonishing number of chin-ups she could do but how completely focused she was on what she was doing. Years later, with great passion and intensity, she shared her thoughts on exercise:

- It is empowering!
- It is fantastic.
- It makes me irresistible.
- I love the physical challenge.
- I feel victorious after I work out.
- It is the fountain of youth!
- I am invincible.

Ximena's Paradigm

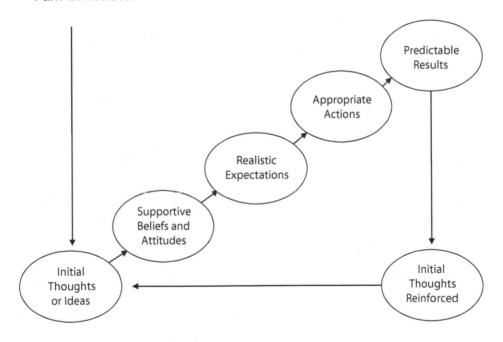

How would you describe Ximena's attitude toward exercise? What would be realistic expectations for a person operating out of that paradigm? Do you think her actions are aligned with her beliefs? What results would you predict for her? All you know about Ximena is how she thinks about exercise. What do you think she looks like? Ximena was crowned Women's Open State Champion, Lightweight Division, of the National Physique Committee (NPC) South Carolina Bodybuilding Championships in 2003 and the NPC South Carolina Excalibur Women's Open Champion, Lightweight Division, in 2006. This would be impressive for anyone at any age; for someone who graduated high school in 1974, it is indeed remarkable. Exceptional people are not the product of average thinking!

Let me update you on Ted. His heart attack could have easily killed him. He is most fortunate to be alive. Since the heart attack, Ted has experienced a paradigm shift, a complete transformation in how he thinks. When I asked how his views on exercise have changed since the heart attack, he answered excitedly that he hadn't missed a day of exercise since leaving the hospital. "As far as priorities go, I equate health and fitness right up there with faith," Ted told me. "Health is the foundation for my day to day life. I just got back from a two-mile walk on the beach!"

Ted's thinking changed completely. Obviously, Ted was capable of thinking this way all along, as I am certain he did not have a brain transplant. Why did it take a near-death experience to think differently? How many people experience this type of transformation but never make it out of the hospital to put their new beliefs into action?

The main purpose of this book is to help you bring about that kind of change. Just like Ted, the power to think differently is within you right now. Exactly how do we go about changing the way we think? Remember, everything begins with a thought, and you have the power to choose how you think.

CHAPTER

7

Personal Inventory

*"Don't it always seem to go
that you don't know what you've got 'til it's gone?
They paved paradise
and put up a parking lot!"*

Big Yellow Taxi
Joni Mitchell

Often, we don't realize just how much we value something until it is too late. It wasn't that health and fitness wasn't important to Ted. After all, getting regular exercise was his New Year's resolution *before* he had the heart attack; it just wasn't important enough. We allow our days to become so filled with "stuff" that we lose sight of what is really important. We take for granted the very things that are dearest to us, and we lose track of our values. If Ted could go back to a point in time before his heart attack, do you think he might reassess the level of priority he placed on health and fitness?

What would you change if you could go back in time? Right now, are you at a point in time before your heart attack? Or maybe you are at the point in time before your wife leaves you, or before you get fired, or before your mother passes away. Wouldn't now be a good time for a personal inventory of values?

Values are the relative worth or importance that we place on specific ideals, ethical principles, character traits, people/relationships, material possessions, and emotions/feelings that make up our human existence. Our values begin to evolve almost from birth, shaped by a variety of influences. For many of us, it is the families we grew up with that have the strongest and most lasting effect on our value systems. As small children, how things are done at home is the only reference we have as to what is right and what is wrong; we can't help but apply "house rules" to the rest of the world. As I discussed in Chapter 4, *Creative Thinking*, the influence our friends have over our value systems cannot be overstated. The culture (group values) we live in is extremely contagious—not necessarily right or wrong, just contagious. We also seem to be subject to genetic predispositions that influence us. It's not that we inherit our values so much as we inherit certain personality traits, and by claiming ownership of these personality traits, we tend to adopt values that support our disposition and discard those that make us uncomfortable.

We all have values, but often they are vague and rarely, if ever, consciously considered. This is not the case for men and women of the highest integrity; they do not suffer from such vagueness. In fact, their high level of integrity is the result of adherence to a carefully considered system of values and principles. Without this deliberate, thoughtful approach in the selection of values, true integrity cannot exist. It is not merely a coincidence that people of the highest integrity also enjoy the highest levels of success. The fact is that you will never find success outside of your value system. What feels like success to one person might feel like torture to another.

Do you believe that Mother Teresa led a successful life? Do you think she could have become a billionaire? What do you think she valued most? Do you believe Donald Trump is successful? Do you believe he would be effective living among and ministering to the poorest of the poor? What do you think he values most?

I hope I get a chance to meet Tiger Woods someday. I have always been impressed with how consistent he is. I am not talking about his model of consistency as a golfer, but as a person. Consistency comes from adherence to values, which is integrity. In an interview with Ed Bradley that originally aired on March 26, 2006, Bradley asked Woods how he thought becoming a father at some point in the future might affect his "day job." Woods replied, "Family always comes first. It always has been in my life, and always will. I may sleep a little bit less, and we have to work on that as a team." In the summer of 2007, Woods and his wife Elin were expecting their first child when Woods was asked what he would do if it seemed likely that Elin would give birth during the Open Championship. In response, the two-time defending Open champion, whose goal since childhood has been to break Jack Nicklaus's record of eighteen major championship wins, stated as a matter of fact, "If she's going to have it the week of the Open, I just won't go." As passionate as Woods is about winning, he values family even more. His success makes clear that we do not have to pursue one value to the exclusion of all others. I believe that long-term success requires some degree of balance.

If we all had the same values in the same order of priority, this world would be a pretty dull place. There would be no political parties, no talk radio, no editorial page, and no spirited debates, and my mother-in-law would never call the conservative TV commentator a jackass. Like I said, dull, dull, dull.

I asked ten people to give me a list of their top twenty-five values, resulting in this list of sixty-three unique values. With such a small sampling, it is likely that you will discover what you consider to be glaring omissions. Carefully review the list and correct any omissions in the space provided.

Family	Making a Difference	Kindness
Community Service	Financial Independence	Generosity
Love	Intelligence	Stability
Accomplishment	Compassion	Attentiveness
Trustworthiness	Passion	Humor
Respect	Creativity	Honor
Tolerance	Wealth	Democracy
Determination	Adventure	Self-Respect
Persistence	Winning	Motivation
Commitment	Health	Gratitude
Honesty	Virtue	Professionalism
Grace	Devotion	Faith
Spiritual Growth	Security	Independence
Sportsmanship	Friendship	Giving
Freedom	Certainty	Pride
Integrity	Success	Serenity
Fairness	Dedication	Humility
Helpfulness	Hard Work	Happiness
Responsible	Wisdom	Recognition
Truth	Joy	Discipline
Perseverance	Perfection	Faithfulness

_____   _____   _____
_____   _____   _____
_____   _____   _____
_____   _____   _____

Once you are satisfied that the values list is complete, circle the ones that you consider to be your top ten or twelve. Now put them in order of priority; for example, if you value your family above everything else, put a small "1" next to the circle. If after family you value security the most, put a small "2" next to the circle, and so on through your top ten values.

Once you have selected the order of your values, transfer your top seven to the list below.

Personal Values List

1. _____

2. _____

3. _____

4. _____

5. _____

6. _____

7. _____

Is this really a list of things you value above all else? Remember, success can be found only within your value system. False humility, political correctness, and popular opinion have no place here. You must be thoughtful and deliberate in choosing that which you value most. You are building a tool for success that is simple but indispensable. Your value system is your compass, providing you with a clear direction under any conditions, a way to keep your bearings.

To complete the next step, you will need whatever tool you use to schedule your time and keep track of your appointments. Excluding sleep, list in descending order how you spent your time over the last four weeks. What activities take up most of your time? Work? Family? Recreation? Don't forget to include unscheduled activities such as watching TV, talking on the phone, and surfing the internet.

Personal Activities List

1. _____

2. _____

3. _____

4. _____

5. _____

6. _____

7. _____

As you compare your Personal Values List and your Personal Activities List, are they aligned? Are you spending most of your time pursuing what you value most? I know that the first time I did this exercise it looked like the lists were created by two different people. My date book was filled with stuff I had to do for other people and void of the things I valued most. Are you having a similar experience right now? It is an easy trap to fall into.

Obviously, I can't see your list, but let me tell you what I know about it. Chances are that you are getting little or no outside pressure to develop your values. No one is going to punish you if you don't follow up with your personal commitment to community service. No one is going make you go running or join the gym, and you won't get fired if you neglect spiritual growth. If you fail to develop your creativity, only you will know. Integrity is a private victory. It is a matter of choice—your responsibility and no one else's.

When I first started developing my value system, I was worried that I would get it wrong. I sensed that this was really important, and I fretted over what order I should put my priorities in. Then it occurred to me that up to this point in my life, I had never even thought about my values, so even if the order wasn't quite right, I had to be better off than I was before! Besides, I have the power to reassess. In fact, I have done just that on more than one occasion.

I have been all over the place regarding money. At one time, whenever I thought about success, I thought only in terms of financial success. The idea was that if I made a lot of money, I would have a successful life. Upon examining my values, I began to see that a truly successful life encompasses a lot more than a fat checking account. As I developed my value system, money got bumped farther and farther down my list. Then, as I continued to work and live within my value system, I realized that I had let the pendulum swing too far the other way. I went from thinking that money means everything to thinking that money was of little importance.

I was wrong on both counts. I now know that money is very important. If you choose to limit yourself financially, you are also choosing to limit yourself in almost every other area of your life. If you value service to your fellow man above all else, you can certainly help more people if you are rich than you can if you are poor. Bill Gates and Warren Buffett, two of the richest men in America, have given billions of dollars to charities[4] over the years. If you don't have it, you can't give it away. Once I began to relax a little regarding money, my income went through the roof.

Imagine that you are able to spend the majority of your time pursuing the things that you value most. Isn't that the purest form of success? Are you ready to align your life with your values to the best of your ability?

Have you ever been on a boat or a plane that had an autopilot? With an autopilot, you can program in where you want to go, and the autopilot will take you there. It is an extremely reliable device, and in most cases it steers far more efficiently than the captain or pilot. The autopilot never gets distracted, tired, or irritated. If you actually watch the helm or the yoke being manipulated by the system, you realize that most of the time you are slightly off course. The autopilot is constantly making small corrections, ensuring that you never stray too far from your intended path. The fact is that we can't help but stray off course from time to time; we are not perfect now and never will be in this life. Much like an autopilot, we need a strong value system to guide us back on track when we lose our way.

The point here is to get your values on paper, to the best of your ability, reflecting things as they stand right now. The following chapters will be meaningless without your Personal Values List. Please resist the urge to start the next chapter until you have completed this one. How many times have you been to a point like this and told yourself "I'll go back and write it down later"? Maybe you really meant to do just that, but somehow you never got around to it. How many times have you read a book or listened to a speaker or audio program without doing the seemingly trivial activities suggested by the author or presenter, and even though the book or program was inspiring and you believed strongly in what you read or heard, lasting change escaped you?

Perhaps those trivial exercises were not so trivial. Are you passionate about creating lasting change in your life? If you are, even though this is hard work, it will be pleasurable work, like gardening is to my friend Vicki. The more you enjoy treasure hunting, the more treasure you will find!

CHAPTER

8

Creating Lasting Change

How many times have you been absolutely committed to changing some aspect of your life, and after much planning and psyching yourself up, you began your new way of life only to revert back to your old self, your old way of doing things, in a matter of days or, in some cases, hours?

The change you sought may well have been tied to one of your highest values, yet you were unable to sustain the effort for any considerable period of time. In Chapter 6, *PreMeditated Model of Success*, we learned that our results merely mirror the way we think. In order to create lasting change, we must first change the way we think. Certainly, you can make slow, plodding improvements by simply changing your actions, but the kind of changes you are seeking, the changes that motivated you to buy this book, can come about only as the result of a shift in how you think. Can the way we think really be changed? Absolutely! Let's examine some of the processes that bring about these radical changes.

Paradigm Shift

The term *paradigm shift* was introduced in 1962 by Thomas Kuhn to describe a change in basic assumptions within the ruling theory of science. In Kuhn's view, the term was limited to the scientific world. The shifts in thinking were global in that one conceptual world view is replaced by another; the entire scientific community adopted new assumptions. Now, Webster's New Millennium Dictionary of English defines a paradigm shift as "a fundamental change in approach or assumptions."

Quantum Leap

Quantum leap is a physics term that has been hijacked by those of us with normal IQs. If you are a quantum physicist, a quantum leap is an abrupt transition of a system described by quantum mechanics from one of its discrete states to another, as the fall of an electron in an atom to an orbit of lower energy. Huh? For those of us from this planet, think of a quantum leap as any sudden and significant change, advance, or increase.

Born Again/Spiritual Awakening

A person who is characterized by a newfound faith or enthusiasm is often referred to as having been *born again*. This shift is brought about by a spiritual experience, or spiritual awakening. Sometimes these experiences come about in the form of sudden, spectacular upheavals in which the person undergoes a profound physic change; his or her entire outlook on life changes almost instantly. Others experience the same results gradually over a period of time.

Epiphany

An epiphany is a sudden, intuitive perception of or insight into the reality or essential meaning of something, usually initiated by some simple or commonplace occurrence or experience.

Life-Changing Event

We can all relate to the effects of a life-changing event. Whether it is a health issue, a divorce, the birth of a child, the death of a loved one, getting fired from a job or cut from a team, we have all experienced these situations, or at least thought about how we might react to them.

A life-changing event, such as my friend Ted experienced with his health, is an easy sell to your peers. No one challenges the radical transformation that happens before their eyes; it makes sense to them. If you total your car and nearly kill yourself while driving drunk, even your most hard-core drinking buddies are supportive when you check yourself into rehab. Even if we, ourselves, have been unable to quit smoking, we are confident that our friend with lung cancer can give up the cigarettes. We are confident because we know we could stop too, *if we had cancer.* A life-changing event fits the way most of us think already. Perhaps the reason that shifts in thinking associated with these types of events often last a lifetime lies in the fact that our culture (group values) allows for that kind of change. An epiphany, spiritual awakening, and other forms of sudden change don't always offer a point of reference that our peers can relate to. Without a paradigm shift of their own, they just can't see what you see. The reason our peers feel threatened by the changes in us is that sometimes our old friends get left behind as we move in new directions. It's the effect your change has on their lives, not yours, that concerns them.

Moving forward in a new direction is critically important if you want your new way of thinking to take root. You must take action based on your new way of thinking or your moment of clarity will dim; your new vision for your life will die. Your actions will determine you.

I know this appears to be in direct conflict with everything you have read to this point, but if you will bear with me a minute longer, you will see there is no inconsistency in this model, no paradox to wrap your mind around. Remember that the call to action here is based on your new way of thinking, your new paradigm. The only way you have of reinforcing your new beliefs is through the results of the actions you take. This is how "belief" in something evolves into "faith" in something.

You might come to believe that exercise is the fountain of youth and that it will make you irresistible, but until you take action on that belief and experience what it is like to be irresistible, you will not have faith that it is true. If you do not act on your beliefs, they will die.

> *"Faith can move mountains,*
> *but bring a shovel."*
>
> **Unknown**

What if you have not experienced a paradigm shift, quantum leap, spiritual awakening, or an epiphany; been born again; or gone through a life-changing experience? What if there is no *new way of thinking* to take action on? What if you are unable to break free of your current frame of reference long enough to make any progress along these lines? Is there any way to move forward under these circumstances?

The answer is yes, provided that you are willing to accept the premise that change is possible. Once you open yourself up to the possibility of change, you have already begun to change.

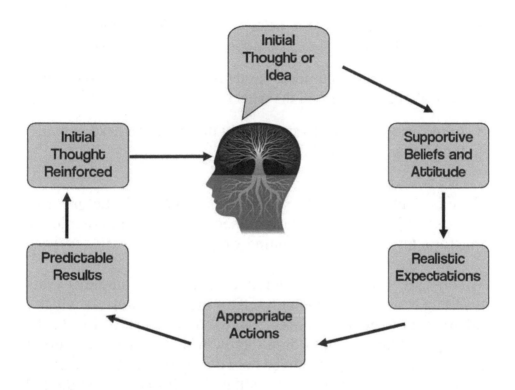

Here is how you start using the PreMeditated Model of Success as your guide:

- Adopt the initial idea or thought that transformational change is possible.

- Embrace the attitude and belief that you are responsible for your thoughts and that you can choose what you will allow to influence you.

- Know in your heart that it is realistic to expect great success as a result of your new way of thinking.

- Immediately begin a program of appropriate actions deliberately designed to create a paradigm shift within you.

- Celebrate your progress; acknowledge how accurately your attitudes, beliefs, and expectations predicted your results.

- Use your reinforced ideas to build momentum, powering through the next turn on the wheel.

- Immediately start a new cycle, only this time you have faith in the idea and the initial thought.

I love this stuff. I love it because it changed my life. Let me give you a specific example of how I used this model to completely transform my ideas about building wealth.

After twenty years in the restaurant business and a couple of years of selling real estate, I found myself sitting in a seminar at which I did not want to be. I had never been exposed to professional self-development before, and I didn't know what to expect. On top of that, the seminar happened to be held during one of those once-in-a-decade snowfalls that we get on the Carolina coast, and the kid in me really wanted to go outside and play in the snow. Mustering every ounce of maturity I possessed, I showed up, on time, determined to make the best of it. I have often wondered since what direction my life might have taken if I had decided to play hooky that day and throw snowballs at cars.

The facilitator, Myers Barnes[5], was excellent, and yes, my sales took off. But the monetary value of my increased commissions was negligible compared to the two new thoughts, or ideas, that I took home with me that day.

The first had to do with reading. Myers mentioned how much he liked to read in his area of expertise. He claimed that if I was willing to read regularly, in about three years I could have a PhD worth of knowledge in my area of interest. The truth is that I have no idea how much you have to read to be equal to a PhD, but I do know that you can go a long way toward becoming an expert in your area of interest simply by reading and applying your new knowledge.

The second concept that struck me that day was the idea that professionally conducted seminars could really shorten my learning curve. Prior to that morning, I never would have considered investing hundreds of dollars, much less thousands of dollars of my own money, to attend a seminar, event, or specialized training. I now view these to be the best return on my time and money. Compared to a traditional college education, the seminars, books, tapes, and CDs I have invested in are a bargain. That's all it took to begin a paradigm shift within me. Here is what happened.

The PreMeditated Model of Success

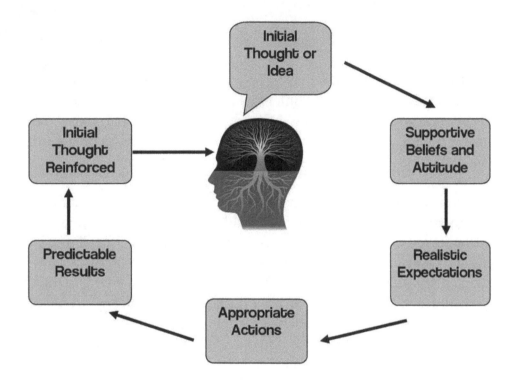

I adopted the initial thought or idea that I could learn how to become wealthy. My attitudes and beliefs began to change immediately; I went from believing that I just didn't quite have what it takes to having an attitude that I have been given everything I need to be successful. My attitudes and beliefs became aligned with my newly adopted thoughts and ideas.

My expectations soared. The belief that I already had within me what it takes to succeed was empowering. I couldn't wait to begin finding and planting wealth-building knowledge; I knew it would bear fruit.

What would be an appropriate action for a person who had the idea that he could learn how to become wealthy, had come to believe that he had been given everything he would need to be successful, and had the high expectation that all necessary knowledge would come quickly and easily? I bought a book—*Rich Dad, Poor Dad*, by Robert Kiyosaki—and I read it!

The results were immediate, and just as my high expectations had predicted, I experienced a shift in how I viewed wealth and becoming wealthy. I learned that forming a corporation would put more money in my pocket even if my sales stayed the same; I learned that most people (the masses) knew very little about acquiring wealth and that I should be careful about to whom I listen; and I raised my standard for what it means to be rich.

I knew that I was on the right path. My initial thoughts and ideas evolved from a belief that this knowledge I sought could be acquired to absolute faith that everything I needed was within my grasp!

I was hungry for more. My next purchase was a book that was first published in 1937, *Think and Grow Rich* by Napoleon Hill. Again, I actually read the book, and as my new beliefs predicted, I was off to the races.

To this day, I am still on the wheel. Over the years, I have built up tremendous momentum. I feel unstoppable. I know that I have within me everything I need to be successful. As long as I stay on this cycle, I will continue to learn *even more* about growing wealth. This doesn't mean that there are never any bumps in the road. As I am writing this book, my primary income source, the real estate market, is experiencing a major correction. The media is filled with reports that the sky is falling. There is a saying that goes something like this: bull markets (real estate or stocks) are born in depression, thrive in recession, and die in euphoria. Some people went broke during the Roaring Twenties, and some people made millions during the Great Depression. Opportunity is ever-present. From firsthand experience, I can tell you that market corrections are not fun when it is your portfolio that is being corrected. Some lessons are painful. There is, however, great comfort in knowing that we are merely between peaks.

I used the example of building wealth because that was my first experience with this phenomenon I now call the PreMeditated Model of Success. I have since learned to use this model in many different areas of my life. All that is required to begin is the premise that change is possible. From there, great things will happen.

CHAPTER

9

A PreMeditated Awakening

I am not sure exactly what time it was, but I think it was around one thirty in the morning when I walked across a bed of hot burning coals in my bare feet. No, I wasn't proving my manhood to the native residents of the Amazon jungle and I wasn't experimenting with hallucinogenic drugs; I was attending a personal development event at the Meadowlands Center in New Jersey. Had I known ahead of time that I would be asked to walk across hot coals, I never would have gone. A day earlier, I would have bet everything I owned that I would never willingly step onto a bed of hot coals burning at 1,200 to 1,800 degrees.

When I was seventeen years old, I was involved in a terrible accident in which a coworker received third-degree burns over approximately a third of her body when I fell down while carrying a ten-gallon pot of boiling water. The fact that I wasn't burned at all is miraculous and the source of tremendous gratitude and guilt.

Even now, I find it difficult to write about that incident. I think how different my life would be today had that boiling water splashed in my face instead of away from me. But even before this happened, walking across a bed of hot coals never once struck me as a good idea. I had seen people do it on TV, and I was positive that it was all staged; I simply did not believe it was possible. There are laws of nature, after all, and one of them is that hot coals will burn you badly. It must be a sham, a hoax, and even if you could do it, why would you? But then I walked across a bed of hot coals, barefoot, no tricks. I didn't get burned. It wasn't that it burned but I could take it or that it burned my skin and I didn't feel it; it just didn't burn. The impossible turned out to be possible. The rules had changed.

On my flight home, I realized how different my thinking had become compared with when I first adopted the idea that I could learn how to become wealthy. Once that idea evolved into the idea that I could learn how to enjoy success in every area of my life, it was just a matter of time before I found myself at the Meadowlands or somewhere similar. After all, attending a personal development seminar is appropriate action for someone who has come to believe that personal development would lead to great success. Once an idea or thought is embraced, the cycle begins.

Now it is time for you to take a spin on the wheel. Choose an area of your life that you have struggled with in the past, an area in which you would like to create lasting change. Do you remember reading about chronic stinking thinking in Chapter 4? When you were reading that paragraph, did a specific area of your life come to mind? Would you like to experience an awakening in this area of your life? Would you like to break the cycle of chronic stinking thinking? This is not snake oil. I am not claiming you will lose thirty pounds in the time it takes you to complete this exercise, that you will suddenly break free of all of the constraints associated with generational poverty, or that this is an effortless quick-fix. If effortless quick-fixes worked, you would have changed things long ago. The fact that you are still reading this book and working the assignments is proof positive that you have what it takes to create lasting change in your life, that you accept the premise that change is possible.

This is an awakening of your own design—*a premeditated awakening.* When I first started down this path, appropriate action for me was reading a single book. As my ideas and thoughts evolved, my appropriate actions evolved to prayer and meditation, reading, listening to books on CD, watching seminars on DVD, flying across the country to attend live events, teaching the principles of success to others, and eventually writing this book. When I began, I wasn't capable of the initial thought or idea that I could write a book. My paradigm didn't allow for such nonsense. It was through working the PreMeditated Model of Success that my paradigm shifted. I evolved. Every time I went around the cycle again, I built momentum. My conception of what was possible expanded, and new features appeared on my map.

Are you ready to initiate a premeditated awakening?

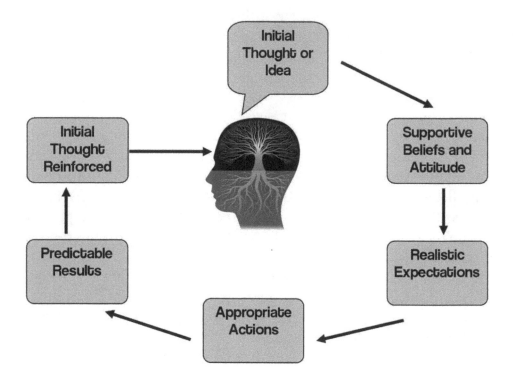

The area of my life in which I must create lasting change is:

_____

_____

I am now willing to accept the premise that change is possible and that I am responsible!

A PreMeditated Awakening

I have adopted the new thought or idea that _____

_____

_____

_____.

Choose an empowering thought or idea. Instead of the thought "I can get in shape," try "I can enjoy the energy and confidence that is the natural result of being physically fit." Instead of "I can make more money," try something like "I can enjoy the freedom of financial independence." Express your thoughts and ideas in a powerful and exciting manner that inspires you.

This new way of thinking is supported by my attitude and belief that _____

_____

_____.

Choose your attitude. Choose your belief. You might finish this statement with something like one of the following: "My new level of fitness draws people to me." "My incredible energy makes me better at everything I do." "I enjoy my life-style of fitness; I never diet and I enjoy exercise!" "Money comes easily and frequently."

It is reasonable for a person with my great attitude and belief system to expect _____

_____

_____.

Examples of reasonable expectations might go something like the following: "to reach my ideal weight range of 170 to 176 pounds," "to complete my first 10K race," "to have the energy to take my grandchildren to Walt Disney World," "to have $10,000 in my savings account," or "for my net worth to exceed two million dollars."

It would be appropriate for a person with these expectations to take these actions: _____
_____
_____.

EXAMPLE:
Let's assume that you have adopted the new thought or idea that "I can enjoy the energy and confidence that is the natural result of being physically fit," you now believe that "my incredible energy makes me better at everything I do," and your expectation is to "complete my first 10K race." Appropriate actions might include these:

- Subscribe to *Runner's World* magazine
- Read Galloway's *Book on Running* by Jeff Galloway
- Find a running/walking partner
- Schedule time for walking and/or running every week
- Locate fun places to run/walk in your area
- Buy a running journal
- Buy new running shoes
- Research what foods are best for runners
- Take the stairs instead of the elevator

This would be a good starting point, the first spin on the wheel. As you build momentum, you will add to your list of actions at the appropriate time. I was in my thirties when I got the idea in my head I could be a runner. Though I couldn't even jog for five minutes without gasping for breath, I believed that it was possible for me to become a runner. I started from where I was, with the simple belief that I could run for five minutes. Once I got to where I could run for five minutes, I started to believe that I could run for ten minutes. I began reading books and magazines about running. Even on the days when running felt hard, I loved how I felt after the run. The first week of January 1994, my average was less than one mile per day. On December 9, 1994, I completed the Kiawah Island Marathon, 26.2 miles, in three hours, twenty-nine minutes, and thirty-four seconds. I have since completed two other marathons, and while I have no plans to run a fourth, "marathoner" will forever be part of my identity. It took me about ten months to prepare myself to run my first marathon; for most people who are in reasonably good health, it is possible to go from nonrunner to marathoner, safely, in about six months.

Whether you are creating lasting change for yourself in the area of fitness, finance, relationships, career, community service, or spiritual growth, at some point it will come down to simply putting one foot in front of the other. As your thinking moves in new directions, your body will follow.

The predictable results of these appropriate actions are

_____

_____

_____.

In the example above, the results would include these:

- I am a runner.

- I have more energy.

- I am noticeably leaner.

- I have a written training plan to complete a 10K.

- I have selected the date and location of my first race.

- I run routinely as part of my lifestyle.

- I make healthy food choices, but I do not diet.

My initial ideas and thoughts have been confirmed. I now believe… (begin the next cycle)

Notice how consistent the results are with the initial thought or idea that began the cycle. Once you see yourself as a runner and experience the new level of energy, it is reasonable for your expectations to grow. Your only restriction is your own imagination.

The true sign of intelligence is not knowledge but imagination."

Albert Einstein

Please check out the Message Board at www.premeditatedsuccess. com and share your empowering thoughts and ideas with others. Discover what appropriate actions others have taken to enjoy the results you desire. Download the PreMeditated Awakening Guide to create lasting change in any area of your life.

CHAPTER

10

The Rules of Life

O ver the years, I have intentionally immersed myself with some of the best personal development facilitators, coaches, and mentors on this planet. I have hired personal fitness trainers, management consultants, and even a writing coach. I have attended their events, read their books, listened to tapes and CDs, and watched DVDs. I am coached by people I have never been in the same room with via email and phone. There have been times that I have made quantum leaps, sudden and profound shifts in my thinking, and there have been times that I simply captured a new thought or idea that led me to an awakening. I know if I change my thoughts, my actions will change.

Therefore, I focus my actions on things that will move my thoughts in the direction of my choosing. It is this circular connection between our thoughts and our actions that bring about our reality. Remember that all creations begin with thought. If you want to create lasting change in your actions, you must first create lasting change in your thinking.

One of the most thought-altering books I have ever read is *The 7 Habits of Highly Effective People* by Stephen R. Covey. I read this book for the first time very early in my personal development. Much of the vocabulary and terms were new to me, and it took a real commitment on my part to read the entire book at a pace that allowed me to comprehend what I was reading. Covey made it clear that in order for me to get the most out of the seven habits, I must teach them to others, and it was through teaching that I began to fully integrate them into my life.

Although new to me, these concepts have been around almost as long as men have been recording history. It was while working the seven habits that I first committed to paper my principles, or what Covey described as a Personal Mission Statement. By carefully choosing my values and principles, I created the standard by which I would hold myself accountable. Although I am far from perfect in the application, the idea is to conduct myself based on my principles rather than my impulses. Integrity, in my case, would be measured by my adherence to my mission statement.

My mission in life is to:
(My principles require that I)

- Continually seek God's will for me and to be free of self-centeredness

- Be kind and helpful to all I encounter

- Treat the individual with dignity and respect

- Have my actions express my principles and values

- Be a reliable source of love, comfort, and understanding for my wife and children

- Have fun with my wife and children

- Teach my children my guiding principles

- Keep my promises

- Be a dependable son and brother who is available and empathetic

- Be a good friend

- Be a contributor in my community, generously giving my time and money

- Encourage others

- Do good work

- Play hard

- Improve my mental and physical capacities daily

- Be open minded to changes and new ideas while having changeless values and principles

A mission statement is a statement of principles. Principles are the rules or standards of behavior we adopt for ourselves. Although principles are shaped by values, they are not the same as values. I *value* my family and relationships. To be a reliable source of love, comfort, and understanding for my wife and children is a *principle* to which I hold myself accountable. Principles are rules for my behavior and are never dependent on the actions of others. My standard of treating people with dignity and respect places the responsibility and control of my life squarely on my shoulders. It is easy for me to treat people with dignity and respect when things are going my way and the people I am dealing with are respectful.

The challenge for me is when I am under extreme pressure and the person in front of me is indifferent or disrespectful.

This is precisely where my principles, or a strong sense of mission, are of extreme value. If I can choose ahead of time, before the bullets are flying overhead and the pot's boiling over, exactly how I want to respond in these circumstances, I am much less likely to react impulsively. It is in my ability to choose how I will respond that gives me my greatest freedom.

A mission statement is not the kind of thing that you can knock out in five minutes before moving on to the next chapter. It is the product of deliberate, thoughtful consideration. A mission statement or, if you prefer, a statement of principles is a powerful tool in achieving premeditated success in life. How we conduct ourselves and how we respond is done deliberately, planned in advance. This is the most effective way to take charge of your life.

While the changes that occurred in my life as the result of working through and teaching the 7 Habits were spectacular when compared with when I first picked up the book, they were not sudden, dramatic upheavals. It was a matter of introducing new thoughts and ideas into the PreMeditated Model of Success and allowing each cycle to change me a little, day in and day out. My new standards and principles developed slowly over a period of time.

But that's not how the rules associated with my values were overhauled. Here I experienced a sudden, dramatic quantum leap that forever changed my thoughts and ideas surrounding my value system. During the course of a five-day seminar I was attending, a family of four went through an intervention, on stage, before a crowd of about 2,500 participants. The parents had been separated, and the younger of the two daughters, a fifteen-year-old, had been threatening suicide. I identified strongly with the father as he talked about how much he valued his family, explaining what it takes for him to feel good about his family, saying things like "Everyone is happy," "Everyone is in a good mood all of the time," "There is never any fighting or arguing," and "They are all smiling." It sounded like utopia to me. Unfortunately, it could never truly be utopia. He lives with three women—how often do you think everyone is really happy, all smiles, not fighting or arguing, or in a good mood? Could it ever be that way *all of the time*? It was nearly impossible for him to feel good about his family. His highest value was a consistent source of disappointment.

I immediately saw where I had been doing the same thing in many areas of my life. I had set myself up to fail in the areas that meant the most to me. I could hardly contain myself. If I am going to be reasonably happy most of the time, I must be able to easily align myself with that which I value most. Whereas my principles, by design, offer very little in the way of wiggle room, my values and the rules surrounding them require a broad path.

In some cases, I had unconsciously become dependent on the actions of others to feel success within my value system. In other cases, my rules made no allowances for human imperfection. I had an all-or-nothing approach to almost everything. When we are talking about the things we value most in life, an all-or-nothing approach doesn't make much sense, does it? Here are a few examples of my old rules.

Old Rules for Health and Fitness

- I run every day.

- I lift weights three days a week.

- I eat only healthy foods.

- I never eat desserts.

- My weight never exceeds 168 pounds.

It was all or nothing. I might run eighty or ninety days in row, but if I missed just one day, I felt like I had blown it. Instead of starting back the next day, I waited until I was psyched up to run every day again. If I missed a workout, it was all over. I could eat perfectly for two weeks, have ice cream for dessert, and completely abandon my diet. Even though I had done really well for twenty-seven out of twenty-eight meals, I had failed. I just didn't have enough self-discipline (self-punishment) to succeed.

Old Rules for Family

- Joyce (my wife) is happy.

- Joyce *is in the mood* whenever *I'm in the mood.*

- No one is arguing.

- My sons are happy.

- My sons are not in trouble.

- No one is complaining about anything.

You can see how I was able to relate to the father in the previous example so easily. You know what I've learned? Sometimes my wife enjoys a good argument or likes being in a sour mood. The majority of the time it has nothing to do with me. And unlike men, women don't think about sex every minute of every day. How strange is that? Furthermore, my children do in fact behave like children from time to time; so do I, for that matter. I have a tendency to interpret complaints as failures on my part. I never liked failing very much. Based on my old rules, do you think family was more likely to be a source of pleasure or disappointment?

Here are some examples of how my rules have evolved:

New Rules for Health and Fitness

I enjoy the gift of health and fitness whenever I make healthy food choices, or I run for ten or more minutes, or I walk on the beach, or I choose to take the stairs, or I lift weights, or I do twenty-five or more push-ups, or I do twenty-five or more crunches, or I park far away from the door, or I go surfing, or I go kayaking, or I go sailing, or I drink plenty of water, or I weigh between 168 and 176 pounds, or when my energy fills the room.

Every day, I enjoy success in health and fitness. I am no longer walking on a tightrope. The truth is that one bad meal a week will not make me unhealthy any more than one good meal a week would make me healthy. If I miss a day of running, it is not the end of the world. Now, if I am training for a race or a specific goal, I may be much stricter with my guidelines, but for everyday living I want to set myself up to succeed.

New Rules for Family

I enjoy the gift of Family whenever I have fun with my family, or I am their number one raving fan, or I am their sounding board, or I am contagiously enthusiastic, or I am the dream fulfillment center, or I am Joyce's sugar daddy, or I am their best friend, or I am the wise and patient teacher, or I am the Magnificent Mood Dispenser, or I am their rock of support.

Referring to page 43, list your top five values along with your old rules for success.

Top Five Values (Old Rules)

1. _____
   _____
   _____
   _____

2. _____
   _____
   _____
   _____

3. _____
   _____
   _____
   _____

4. _____
   _____
   _____
   _____

5. _____

_____

_____

_____

_____

Now let's have some fun. Using your imagination, create new rules for each of your top five values. Make sure the rules are for how you act and feel, not for how other people act or feel. Give yourself plenty of ways to succeed in each value. You should be thinking to yourself "I can do that" as you write down each of your new rules. Give yourself superhero status if necessary. Grumpy people are no match for the Magnificent Mood Dispenser!

I enjoy the gift of _____ **whenever**

_____

_____

_____

_____

_____

_____

I enjoy the gift of _____ **whenever**

_____

_____

_____

_____

_____

_____

I enjoy the gift of _____ whenever

_____

_____

_____

_____

_____

_____

I enjoy the gift of _____ whenever

_____

_____

_____

_____

_____

_____

I enjoy the gift of _____ whenever

_____

_____

_____

_____

_____

_____

When I was walked through this process at "Date with Destiny," an Anthony Robbins event, I was filled with a sense of freedom and purpose. A burden I never knew I was carrying was lifted from me. My view of the world had changed. I fully understood that happiness is an inside job.

"Great things are done by a series of small things brought together."

Vincent Van Gogh

CHAPTER

11

A Front-End Alignment

O ne night, while dining at a local restaurant, I decided I was going to learn how to windsurf. It was the bartender Chris, an expert at windsurfing, who inspired me to take up the sport. When he is in the water, crowds of spectators form on the beach, oohing and ahhing as he performs tricks in the surf. He is obviously having a lot fun, and he makes it look easy.

Being that I loved sailing and surfing, windsurfing seemed like a no-brainer for me. So when he suggested I learn, I jumped at the chance. True to my "go for it" personality, I ordered all brand-new equipment, purchased a few books and videos, and arranged for Chris to give me lessons.

For me, the learning curve for windsurfing was huge. It was really hard work—so much so that I would come home whipped with my hands bleeding and my back aching. Learning to windsurf just wasn't that much fun, but I stuck with it. I figured that once I obtained a certain level of competency, I would start to enjoy myself.

I kept at it until, finally, the day came that I could plane, jibe, tack, and water-start; I could sail right off the beach through the breakers, and on days when there wasn't much else to see, I could draw my own modest crowd of semi-awestruck spectators. There was only one small problem. I still wasn't having any fun. I simply did not enjoy windsurfing. I know this sounds dumb, but I had a really hard time accepting the fact that I didn't like what I was doing. I had so much time, money, and energy invested that quitting just didn't seem right. What would my wife say about all that money I spent? What would my friends think about my sudden about-face regarding windsurfing? So I kept at it, imagining somehow I would reach a point that it would magically become fun. I would try different places, different conditions, all with the same result. It wasn't until after an un-fun day of windsurfing in Aruba (the windsurfing capital of the world) that I finally came to the conclusion that it was time to give it up.

A hobby that plays out like this it is no big deal. It is, after all, discretionary time, but when this scenario arises in your career, marriage, or other long-term relationships, it can rob you of years of happiness. I remember how difficult it was for me to leave the restaurant business. For sixteen of the twenty years I worked in the industry, I really enjoyed what I was doing. I worked with interesting people from a variety of backgrounds. We employed everyone from Duke University students (many of whom are doctors today) waiting tables during their summer break to the functionally illiterate living paycheck to paycheck.

As the company grew, so many new areas of responsibility arose that I was constantly learning new skills. My entire social network was built around people I met in the food service industry, including my wife, whom I met one summer while she was waiting tables as a college student. To a much greater extent than I like to admit, my job was my identity.

Once the company stopped expanding and it became obvious that tomorrow was going to look pretty much the same as today, the job started to weigh on me. I began to resent having to work every weekend. I didn't know what it was like to sit down and have dinner with my family at night. I came to believe that anyone who was willing to work as hard as I was working could and should make a lot more money than I was being paid. Still, with all of the time and energy I had invested, it took me four years after I became unhappy to work up the courage to leave.

My good friend and business mentor Grant Hollett taught me the perils of the Sunk Money Syndrome. The Sunk Money Syndrome occurs when businesses decide to hang onto systems and initiatives that are losing money or failing to meet objectives simply because of the amount of money they had already sunk into the project. I learned to disregard sunk money when making decisions for the future of my business, focusing instead on what is best for the business from this point forward. The underlying concept of the Sunk Money Syndrome applies to other areas of my life.

Continuing to spend my time and energy in ways that are clearly not meeting my objectives simply because I have so much time and energy invested (sunk) only ensures that my future will look like my past. Whether it is a hobby, my career, or a relationship that is robbing me of my most precious resource (my time), I must forget sunk money and move on.

What is life beyond how we spend our time? You cannot describe a person's life without describing how that person spends the hours of his or her days. Try it. Describe someone else's life. Are you describing how that person spends (or spent) time? Are you talking about his or her actions or intentions? It is funny how we consider things like good intentions and motives when we describe our own lives, but we judge everyone else by their actions.

Don't feel badly; you are being judged the same way. You may consider your motives and good intentions to be the real you, but the truth is that the real you is your actions. It is what you do, not what you meant to do, that defines you. Your life is the way you spend your time. It has been my experience that the people who appear to be enjoying life the most are the people who are spending the most time pursuing their own visions of success.

My good friend Alberta Horn is a great example. Alberta and I worked together for the same real estate company. She was an administrator, and I was a salesperson. After four years, I left the real estate company to open my own office, and she came with me. She was my right hand. I trusted her completely. I have never met anyone with a stronger work ethic. She is great at all of the things at which I really stink. Through all of the pressures of opening a new business and sometimes flying by the seat of our pants, we never had a cross word between us. She was the ultimate team player, the one person who got along with everybody, the go-to person if you had a problem. She never missed a company function and was always the first to sign up for the personal development workshops that I facilitated. It was at one of these workshops that we both realized that it was time for her to go.

Alberta really enjoyed working with me, but the dream of owning a dominant real estate company was my dream, not hers. Her dream was to work with horses. She is a true equestrian. If ever there was a real, honest-to-goodness cowgirl, it is Alberta Horn. She is passionate about horses, gifted in the areas of training horses and teaching young people to ride. When she realized at one of my workshops that she would eventually leave my company, she was reluctant to speak up. Her loyalty to me made her uncomfortable discussing her independent vision of success in a room filled with my employees and associates. I was excited for her. Though she could not clearly see how she was going to build a career around horses, I had no doubt that it would come about. At first she thought maybe a career as a large-animal veterinarian assistant might be the way, but what she got was even better.

In less than a year, Raisin' Kain Ranch was in full operation. I speak with Alberta often, and she has never been happier. In addition to her own horses, she boards fifteen additional animals. She gives riding lessons, trains horses, competes at horse shows, and coaches other riders. She is working harder than she ever has and loves every minute of it. Once Alberta became clear on what she wanted, everything fell into place.

So how are you spending your life? Whose visions of success are you pursuing, yours or someone else's? Are you still struggling to windsurf when you really want to be riding a horse? Have you fallen into the self-made trap of the Sunk Money Syndrome? Now is a good time to revisit your Personal Vision of Success. Referring to page 7, transfer your Personal Vision of Success onto the following lines.

I enjoy great success in life now that...

- _____
- _____
- _____
- _____
- _____
- _____
- _____
- _____
- _____
- _____

IMPORTANT NOTE:

I am going to walk you through a simple process that will enable you to zero in on what areas of success matter most to you. Follow these instructions carefully. Resist the urge to "wing it" or take shortcuts. Remain diligent. You are just a few steps away from building an amazing tool for success, assembled from the assignments you have completed in this book. Your Personal Vision of Success must become crystal clear. Murky vision yields murky results. DO NOT rush through this; think accuracy, not speed.

Begin by comparing your first two statements. If you could enjoy only one of these two areas of success, which one would it be?

EXAMPLE:
I enjoy great success in life now that...

- My real estate company is number one in market share

- I enjoy vibrant health and fitness

- My book is a national best seller

- I spend my winters on my sailboat in the Caribbean

- I live on oceanfront property

In this example, I would be comparing "My real estate company is number one in market share" with "I enjoy vibrant health and fitness." My choice of those two would be vibrant health and fitness. Now I compare vibrant health and fitness with "My book is a national best seller"—I still choose health and fitness. I continue down the list, choosing vibrant health and fitness over sailing in the Caribbean and then again over living on oceanfront property. At this point, I know that health and fitness is the most important area in my life for me to enjoy success. I write "I enjoy vibrant health and fitness" on the first line of my prioritized list and cross it off my old list.

EXAMPLE:
I enjoy great success in life now that...

- My real estate company is number one in market share

- ~~I enjoy vibrant health and fitness~~

- My book is a national best seller

- I spend my winters on my sailboat in the Caribbean

- I live on oceanfront property

EXAMPLE:
I enjoy great success in life now that...
(In order of priority)

- I enjoy vibrant health and fitness

_____

_____

_____

_____

Now I start over with the remaining areas of success. If I could have only one, would I rather have my real estate company be number one or my book be a national best seller? Once I have decided on the best seller, I compare writing a best seller to sailing the Caribbean, again choosing the best seller. Now I compare writing a best seller to living on oceanfront property. In this example, I have selected "My book is a national best seller" as my next priority for success in life. I transfer my selection and cross it off my list.

EXAMPLE:
I enjoy great success in life now that...

- My real estate company is number one in market share

- ~~I enjoy vibrant health and fitness~~

- ~~My book is a national best seller~~

- I spend my winters on my sailboat in the Caribbean

- I live on oceanfront property

EXAMPLE:
I enjoy great success in life now that...
(In order of priority)

- I enjoy vibrant health and fitness

- My book is a national best seller

_____

_____

_____

Continue with this process until you have all ten areas of success listed in order of priority.

Personal Vision of Success

I enjoy great success in life now that... *(In order of priority)*

- _____
- _____
- _____
- _____
- _____
- _____
- _____
- _____
- _____
- _____

During the proofreading of this chapter, it was suggested that it might be difficult for some people new to this process to relate to the examples I used. It struck me just how far I have come in such a short period of time. A few years ago, owning my own business, writing a book, and living on oceanfront property were all beyond my wildest dreams. Now, I fully expect to enjoy that level of success in every area of my life. Whether your vision is to own your own company, become the top salesperson or simply get a job, live near the ocean, or move into your own apartment, make sure your vision moves you forward. Consider your vision of success carefully as you answer the following questions:

What does this level of success feel like?

_____

_____

_____

Why is this worth pursuing?

_____

_____

_____

_____

_____

Will your pursuit of success in these areas be a labor of love or forced hard labor? Why?

_____

_____

_____

_____

_____

Is your vision of success consistent with your values? How?

_____

_____

_____

_____

Remember, if you want it all, you can have it all. It's entirely up to you. Are you ready to make a decision? Is today the day? How will you begin to enjoy great success in life right now?

_____

_____

_____

_____

_____

Once you make a decision, the universe conspires to make it happen."

Ralph Waldo Emerson

CHAPTER

12

Passionate Disbelief

"There is a principle which is a bar against all information, which is proof against all arguments and which cannot fail to keep a man in everlasting ignorance—that principle is contempt prior to investigation."

Herbert Spencer

Oprah Winfrey is the Emmy Award–winning host of the highest-rated talk show in television history. She is an Academy Award–nominated actress, a magazine publisher, a self-made billionaire, and by some assessments the most influential woman in the world. She is among the truly remarkable, and whenever the truly remarkable speak of success, I listen carefully. During an interview with Larry King that aired on May 1, 2007, Oprah openly discussed her long-held belief in the law of attraction and how she used it to draw the movie *The Color Purple* into her life in 1985. While stating, as a matter of fact, that you really can change your own reality based on the way that you think, she went on to make the point that the law of attraction is just one law; it is not the answer to all questions. There are other laws and other factors to consider.

To many people, the law of attraction is a relatively new theory that received tremendous exposure in the 2006 movie *The Secret*[6]. The law of attraction states that our predominant thoughts and feelings become physical manifestations, thereby giving us direct control over our reality through the power of thought. In other words, our thoughts determine our physical experience. Sound familiar? It should. Proponents and critics of the law of attraction have been around for centuries. Some people eagerly embrace these concepts as their long-sought solution to creating positive change in their lives, while others are as passionate in their disbelief.

It is understandable why some people have a difficult time buying into this idea. The law of attraction places the responsibility for one's life squarely on the shoulders of the believer. If you have spent the majority of your life playing the role of the victim and blaming other people and circumstances for your lot in life, this idea can be very difficult to accept. For many, it is easier to disbelieve the law of attraction and abandon the idea of ever enjoying success than it is to question their lifelong beliefs and attitudes.

For some people, even the slightest suggestion that the victims of violent crimes and sexual abuse somehow brought that upon themselves is just cause to reject the concept without further investigation. Others ask, How does a person attract cancer, multiple sclerosis, a brain aneurysm, or other afflictions? What did that newborn baby do to attract blindness? Can my illness really be tied to the way I think?

Others struggle with anything outside the strict doctrine of their church or religious culture. I have seen different people of the same religious sect embrace and reject the law of attraction based on their spiritual beliefs. Among the more secular critics are those who question the so-called scientific fact that every thought puts out its own specific vibration to which the universe responds. How can the proponents of the law of attraction call something a scientific fact if it cannot be tested or observed? Some agnostics are put off by the spiritual nature of the law, while at the same time some people who view life from a spiritual perspective are put off by the scientific-metaphysical explanations.

If you are looking for a reason to disbelieve the law of attraction, you should have little trouble coming up with one. I do not pretend to have the answer to every question, nor do I believe that the law of attraction is the answer to every question. How, then, does the skeptic—faced with these legitimate questions and doubts and lacking measurable, observable proof—come to believe in this power that can bring about lasting change?

All that is required is an open mind. To make a start, you do not have to believe; you just have to be willing to believe. When you consider the broad mix of people who have referenced concepts consistent with the law of attraction—including spiritual leaders, scientists, teachers, speakers, authors, Nobel Prize winners, philosophers, biblical authors, Buddha, Confucius, Henry David Thoreau, Ralph Waldo Emerson, Albert Einstein, Dale Carnegie, Napoleon Hill, George Bernard Shaw, Wallace Wattles, Henry Ford, Earl Nightingale, Bob Proctor, Jack Canfield, and many other remarkably successful people—doesn't it seem foolish to simply dismiss it without investigation?

One of the more common stumbling blocks that I have come across when working with others is the oversimplification or misinterpretation of the law itself, building a model of success that looks like this:

THOUGHTS and FEELINGS

↓

RESULTS (REALITY)

To say that what we are experiencing now is the result of our thoughts and feelings is a true statement; however, it is misleadingly incomplete. In my opinion, the contributors to *The Secret*, in an effort to emphasize the importance of our thoughts and feelings and the dominant effect they have over our lives, undersold the need to take action consistent with our new way of thinking. When you look at the list of contributors to *The Secret*, you can see that they are all people of action, yet the need to take action was not emphasized.

It first becomes evident that you have indeed changed your thinking when you notice that your actions have changed with very little effort on your part. I know the law of attraction exists. I know it exists because I have experienced it. I changed my reality by first changing the way I think. *Pay close attention here.* I did not say I changed my reality *just* by changing the way I think; I said I changed my reality by *first* changing the way I think.

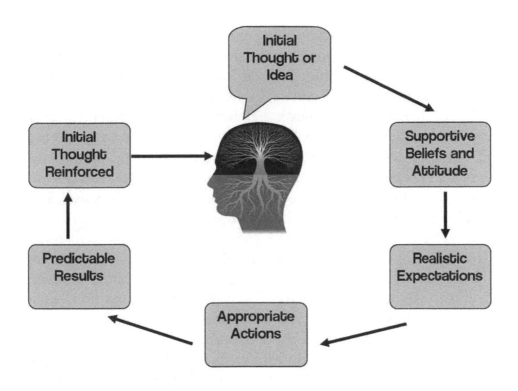

It is the law of attraction that begins the PreMeditated Model of Success, but it is just the beginning. Predictable results follow appropriate actions.

Some proponents of the law of attraction claim that all of the bad stuff you are experiencing in life is the direct result of what you have thought and attracted. Does this mean that all of the people who are hungry and living in poverty have brought that upon themselves?

Without question, generational poverty is an incredibly difficult cycle to break. When children are born into famine and poverty, it is all they know. It is all their parents knew; it is all their grandparents knew. How do children in these homes ever get exposed to a way of thinking that can lift them from this situation? I imagine that the thoughts and talk among them is of poverty and hunger, which only attracts more poverty and hunger. Apply this line of thinking to the PreMeditated Model of Success: "**Thinking** about how poor and hungry I am leads to an **attitude** of despair and a **belief** that things will never get better. I don't **expect** to ever rise above this; my father didn't, his father didn't, why should I? The best **action** for me is to quit school and hustle by the best way I can. The earning opportunities for a street kid with a fifth-grade education aren't enough to feed and clothe me [**results**]. I'm **thinking** my kids and I sure are poor and hungry."

There is an old saying among Texas oil speculators that goes something like this: "There is no shame in going broke, but don't ever, ever say you are poor!" "Broke" is a temporary condition, what some call situational poverty; to be poor infers permanence, or generational poverty. Do I think children attracted the poverty they were born into? Certainly not. I do believe, however, that those living in generational poverty will be unable to change their reality unless they experience a profound change in the way they think.

What about diseases and poor health? Have people with cancer attracted cancer to themselves? I don't know, but I do know that our health is greatly affected by the way we think. Are you familiar with placebos? A placebo is an inactive substance or preparation used as a control in an experiment or test to determine the effectiveness of a medicinal drug.[7]

Those receiving a placebo often get better, a phenomenon known as the placebo effect. In many cases, all a new drug has to do in order to be considered effective is outperform the placebo effect. Why do people taking the placebo improve at a better rate than those taking nothing at all? The answer is simple: they *think* they will get better, they believe they will get better, and the placebo reinforces the patients' expectation that they will get better. Much of the evidence used by proponents of the law of attraction is subjective, lacks testability, and by its very nature is difficult to measure and prove. (How do you measure what a person is thinking and feeling?) This is not the case with the placebo effect, which is a measurable and observable fact of medical science. If the way a person thinks can heal, can it not make that person ill as well? In cultures that believe in black magic, curses are not taken lightly. Just as a placebo can trick a believer into getting well, a curse can trick a believer into getting sick.

It appears that we will all die of something. We do not live forever, at least not in our present form. I don't know how much people's thinking has to do with the acquirement of afflictions, but I do know that their thinking has everything to do with how they deal with it. Some people rise to greatness; others shrink.

Have you ever heard of Jessica Long? She is quite an athlete. In 2006, at the age of fourteen, Jessica swam the 1 Mile Chesapeake Challenge. She finished ninth overall, was the third female finisher overall, and was first in the fourteen and under division. As a competitive swimmer, Jessica has enjoyed extraordinary success. Since 2004, she has been winning trophy after trophy and setting new records. She was a finalist for Sportswoman of the Year in 2006, an award given by the Women's Sports Foundation, and was awarded an Excellence in Sports Performance Yearly award (ESPY) in 2007.

Jessica was born without fibulas, ankles, or heels, and when she was eighteen months old, both of her legs were amputated below her knees. As a swimmer with a disability, Jessica has set thirty-five U.S. records, seventeen pan-American records, two Paralympic records, and fourteen world records. She has won three Paralympic gold medals and nine world championship gold medals.

Do I believe that Jessica attracted the condition that led to her being born without the normal bone structure in her lower legs and feet? Absolutely not. In fact, I passionately disbelieve that. I do believe she attracted the heart, mind, and body of a champion athlete. Jessica has never had physical therapy; "I was determined to do it on my own," she states on her website.[8] She is a champion, I believe, because she thinks like a champion.

Have you ever met a disabled person who was so bitter that everything good in his or her life was overshadowed by the physical imperfection? I ask you, what separates that person from someone like Jessica Long other than the way they think? Isn't it true that those at both extremes live in the reality of their own creation?

Do you want cause for reasonable doubt? Try understanding metaphysics. I always thought it was a branch of science, but it is actually a branch of philosophy that examines the nature of reality, including the relationship between mind and matter.

How about quantum physics or quantum theory? I have read the definitions, and I'm still not sure what they mean. The way I understand it, in the world of quantum theory, everything radiates or vibrates on its own unique frequency. When they say "everything," they mean everything, including our thoughts. When experts in metaphysics and quantum physicists talk about the law of attraction, the talk is about how our thoughts and feelings send out unique vibrations to which the universe responds by manifesting more things in our lives that will make us think and feel the same, thus sending out more of the same vibrations to which the universe responds by manifesting still more things in our lives that create the same feelings and vibrations, which in turn … and so on and so on.

It is a New Age version of "the rich get richer and the poor get poorer." It is hard for me to wrap my mind around all this *thought vibration* stuff. I just don't understand how it works, and fortunately I don't have to.

Do you have cell phone? If not, even an old-fashioned landline phone will do. In the space provided, explain exactly how your phone captures your voice, transmits it through space to be captured by the exact phone that you wanted to receive it, and then reproduces your voice so clearly that the person you called knows it's you before you can identify yourself. How exactly does that work?

_____

_____

_____

_____

_____

Did I give you enough space? Could you even begin to explain how it works? Does your lack of understanding interfere with your ability to use a phone? I have found the law of attraction to be just as user-friendly as my cell phone. I don't have to understand how it works; I just had to learn how to use it.

I love a good paradox. According to the law of attraction, if you think there is no proof that the law exists, you will attract no proof that the law exists. If you are looking for reasons to disbelieve, you will find them, and likewise, if you are looking for reasons to believe, they are all around you.

"Whether you think you can, or you think you can't, you are right."

Henry Ford

CHAPTER

13

PreMeditated Insubordination

Time is the most precious of all our resources. Every great personal development program I have ever studied includes some element of time management. I find the study of time management fascinating. I was once convinced that I was unusually challenged in this area, but I have since come to believe that many people share the same time management issues as I do.

I have tried time management quadrants, prioritized checklists, color-coded files, electronic reminders, clipboards, tape recorders, personal assistants, Palm Pilots, leather-bound day-planners, thousands of sticky notes, string tied to my finger, tapes, seminars, and countless books, all in an effort to manage my time more effectively.

My results were terrible. I felt as if there just wasn't enough time to do everything I wanted, and needed, to do. With each failed experiment, my frustration grew. It wasn't until I became crystal clear on my values, my principles, and my personal vision of success that I began to make progress in this area. With clarity of purpose, I experienced a profound shift in the way I viewed time management, enabling me to finally take charge of my life.

The phrase *time management* is a bit of a misnomer. Time itself cannot be managed. It is beyond our control and direction; we cannot produce more of it to meet demand and we cannot conserve it to make it last longer. We can't save some for later. It is impossible for us to not spend time. Time marches on; it waits for no one. If you are running short on time, it is not because someone else has more than their fair share. Time is the one resource that is distributed evenly. From the most productive among us to the least, we all work with a twenty-four–hour day.

Humans seem to have a difficult time imagining things coming to an end. We label the most reckless among us as living like there is no tomorrow, but I suspect they are more living as if there is an endless supply of tomorrows, believing there will be time down the road to do what they value most and to right any wrongs.

In our logical minds, we know our resources are not limitless—that someday we will run out of oil, that the fish in the sea are numbered, and that eventually our lives will draw to a close. We know these things intellectually, but we can't really visualize them. Can you even imagine *not being*? Doesn't it *feel* like we will be here forever? It is this illusion of permanence that makes us sloppy consumers of time. The false belief that somehow we will have more time in the future defies all logic. At the rate of sixty minutes per hour, twenty-four hours per day, our lives are irreversibly consumed. Time management is not about saving time or slowing down the rate at which our time is spent; it is about choosing how we consume it.

Let's examine some statistics gathered from the *American Time Use Survey* conducted by the U.S. Department of Labor, Bureau of Labor Statistics, regarding working parents.

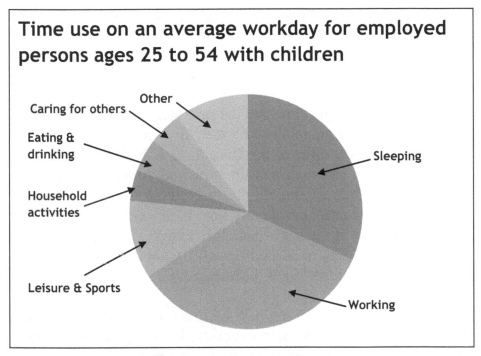

Time use on an average workday for employed persons ages 25 to 54 with children

SOURCE: Bureau of Labor Statistics

I selected this specific demographic to illustrate that even on working days, the busiest among us have a significant amount of time available for "choose to" activities. Throughout this chapter, we will be referring to the activities we engage in as either "choose to" activities, as in a matter of choice, or "have to" activities, referring to activities that must be done whether you want to do them or not.

Have-to activities are either imposed upon you by nature or are integrity-based "musts," self-imposed through strict adherence to your values and principles. Sleep, for example, is a natural law, a have-to activity. The amount of sleep people require ranges from as little as five hours to as much as ten hours, with most healthy people averaging between seven and eight hours of sleep each day. Over any significant period of time, you will meet your sleep requirements. You really have no choice. Your survival instinct will see to it that you comply with natural law, but what about the integrity-based have-to activities?

Let's look at the biggest piece of the pie: work. The parents in this survey spend more than a third of their lives at work, but do they have to work? According to the Bureau of Labor Statistics, there were 7.2 million (4.7 percent) unemployed Americans of working age reported during the month of October 2007. Historically speaking, this number is relatively low. Most economists consider our nation to be at, or very near, full employment at this level, meaning that just about everyone who wants to work can find employment, if not the job of their dreams.

Considering that even in the best of times there are six to seven million people not working in America, I ask again, do we really *have* to work? The answer for me is yes. To meet my self-imposed obligations and to comply with my values and principles, I *have* to work; in fact, I want to work. Though I consider work to be a have-to activity, the type of work I do and how I align my work with my values and principles is a matter of choice.

For the sake of this discussion, let's avoid all long-winded philosophical debates as to what is a have-to versus a choose-to activity by being extremely conservative in identifying the choose-to activities represented in this pie chart. Let's assume that sleep, work, household activities, eating and drinking, and caring for others are all have-to activities. We are still left with about two and a half hours of leisure and sports time that is purely choose-to time and about two and a half hours of "Other" time that may or may not fall under your control. Let's look at the four primary ways our lives are consumed.

Circumstantial Dictatorships

There are times in everyone's life that circumstances dictate your next move. A situation will arise that requires not only your attention but immediate action as well. When you are under the control of a circumstantial dictatorship, everything else gets pushed aside.

When my friend Ted suffered his heart attack, he didn't stop to consider whether leaving work early would be OK with his supervisor or if stopping by the hospital would make him late for dinner. Circumstances dictated that he immediately seek medical attention. If you wake up in the middle of the night to discover that your house is on fire, you don't turn on the Weather Channel to see how you should dress before going outside.

Circumstantial dictatorships are ruthless; they demand immediate action. They occur whenever something of great value or importance is under immediate threat. These are not limited to life-or-death situations, nor are they always unavoidable. For example, my twelve-year-old son Will is a gifted musician. On a typical Tuesday night, you can find him performing at a local coffee shop, but not last Tuesday. Last Tuesday he was working on a homework project that was due the following morning. Circumstances dictated that he pass up doing what he loves most to get the project done. A school project is a have-to activity, but it didn't become a circumstantial dictatorship until the night before it was due. Will could have invested some of his choose-to time in completing his project in time for him to perform as planned. I admit that I have been guilty of the same thing—putting off important projects at work until they evolve into a circumstantial dictatorship.

Effective time management cannot help you once you find yourself in circumstances beyond your control. It can, however, reduce how often this occurs.

Other People's Priorities

How often have you come home from an extremely busy, stressful day feeling like you have nothing to show for your efforts? When your spouse or significant other asks you what you did all day, you can't really account for your time. You know you were busy, and at the time it felt like you were doing important "stuff," but there was no feeling of satisfaction in a job well done, just fatigue. This is how I feel after a full day of dealing with other people's priorities. Huge chunks of our lives can be spent pursuing other people's priorities, and we don't even realize that it is happening. Sound familiar?

How about this: you interrupt what you are working on to help your favorite coworker fix her computer so she can finish her work. You answer your cell phone while having lunch with your spouse and spend the next thirty minutes trying to get off the phone with your boss. Someone stops by your desk for thirty minutes to tell you all about the company softball game that you didn't attend because you were not interested in the company softball game. You spend the first twenty minutes of your day responding to or deleting unsolicited emails. Someone stops by your house to visit, and because you just don't want to be rude you skip taking your daughter to the mall as promised. Can you proofread this for me? Can you help me with my presentation? Can I ask you a quick question? Would you stop by the store on your way home? Would you drop this off for me? Can you call Bill for me? Will you help with my charity? Can you show me how you did that? Do you know anything about cars? If you are not too busy, I'm looking for volunteers.... Now does it sound familiar?

It's hard to say no, isn't it? Other people's priorities and circumstantial dictatorships both have the appearance of needing to be done right now. Whether real or imagined, there is a certain sense of urgency you feel when responding to other people's priorities. You don't go looking for circumstantial dictatorships or other people's priorities; they come knocking on your door. You feel compelled to take action. You feel like you *have* to open the door. You *have* to answer the phone.

Circumstantial dictatorships involve only the important areas of your life, the areas you value most. Other people's priorities, on the other hand, can have you working hard on things that are of little importance and do nothing to move you toward your vision of success. Where you have to submit to circumstantial dictatorships, you *choose* to submit to other people's priorities.

Frivolous Diversions

Some of our choose-to time is consumed by common, ordinary, seemingly insignificant activities that I refer to as frivolous diversions. Some of the most pleasant times I have ever experienced occurred during the pursuit of these trivial activities. Whether I am sitting on a beach, novel in hand, with no real purpose other than to relax or watching a football game on TV, I find it necessary to incorporate some planned "downtime" into my schedule.

Time away from pressing matters enables me to approach the important areas of my life with renewed vigor and enthusiasm. I choose to make vacations an important part of my life, frivolously spending time and money on a Caribbean island away from my normal routine. In my view, a life that is void of frivolous diversions isn't much of a life at all. I believe we were created to enjoy life, and I make a point of doing just that.

The need to mentally "kick it out of gear" must be satisfied, but when an excessive amount of time is devoted to this, the results can be disastrous. There is no such thing as free time; time gained in one area is time lost in another. Often the very problems and concerns that we are trying to escape through frivolous diversions multiply themselves as we neglect important aspects of our lives. When taken to the extremes, frivolous diversions can rob us of the very freedom we seek. Too much vacation time could lead to loss of income, perhaps even loss of employment, leading to a circumstantial dictatorship in which taking a vacation is no longer an option. Too much party time can take its toll as well. Time spent in the eat-drink-and-be-merry mode is fun every now and then. To just not worry about your cholesterol, your weight, or what all that booze is doing to your body is a feeling of great freedom. But too much time spent at the party will eventually lead to failing health, a circumstantial dictatorship that will dictate exactly what you can and cannot do. Once there, the party's over.

Often it is the people who value their freedom the most that fall victim to this paradox. To them, freedom is the pursuit of frivolous diversions without restraint, and as a result the very freedom they value so highly is taken from them. Circumstances beyond their control dictate their next actions. I find it ironic how often it is those who insist they are free to do as they choose that end up with so few choices.

Life Leadership

Simply put, life leadership is an act of insubordination. I will explain what I mean. When we pursue other people's priorities, we subordinate our own agenda to that of the other person; we *choose* to submit. The same is true of the excesses of frivolous diversions, only in this case it is to our own impulses that we are subordinate. Let's look at what it means to be subordinate:

1. to place in a lower order or rank

2. to make secondary

3. to make subject, subservient, or dependent

When we abandon our own plans in favor of other people's priorities, we acknowledge that our agenda is of less importance; our vision of success is a lower priority than that of the other person. We willingly place ourselves under other people's authority in a position of subservience.

Life leadership is the belief that our own agenda, our values and principles, our Personal Vision of Success, are not of a lower priority than those of other people. Our lives are not of lesser importance. We recognize ourselves as being the leader and authority in our lives. In this respect, our lives are indeed an act of insubordination. We are accountable to ourselves and our own values and principles first and foremost.

Life leadership is the time we invest in the following:

- Developing our values and principles

- Enjoying these things we value most

- Clarifying our Personal Vision of Success

- Pursuing our Personal Vision of Success

Much of this book has focused on the development of your value system and your Personal Vision of Success in life. Life leadership is the *implementation* of your vision. Without effective leadership, leadership that only you can provide, your vision will die of neglect. Often people confuse the desire to be successful with the pursuit of success; life leadership is the pursuit of success.

Before you say, "I'm too busy," or you get the idea in your head that you just don't have the time for this life leadership stuff, understand this: you have all the time in the world available to you. I mean this quite literally. You have all the time in the world; there isn't any more time available to you than the amount you are currently consuming. The only way you can expand the amount of time that you devote to life leadership activities is by shrinking the amount of time that you currently choose to spend serving other people's priorities and indulging in frivolous diversions.

Life Leadership and Other People's Priorities

I would like to clarify that when we are discussing other people's priorities, we are not talking about activities for which you are receiving compensation. If you agree to work in a certain capacity for an agreed-upon wage, while on the job your employer sets the agenda, the job-related priorities are your priorities as well. Your employment should be an enjoyable part of your life in which you meet your objectives as you meet the objectives of your employer. On average, we spend over forty hours a week working. Consider how much life leadership time you gain by incorporating your values and principles into every aspect of your job or by insisting on a work experience that furthers your life's mission. If your employment requires you to engage in activities that conflict with your values and principles or does not move you forward in the pursuit of your Personal Vision of Success, I suggest you seek other employment.

That said, how do we deal with the very real distractions of other people's priorities? For the most part, the other people we are talking about here are not strangers off the street. They are friends, coworkers, family members, neighbors, and acquaintances. Even when it is inconvenient and you really don't want to stop what you are doing, you feel compelled to assist them. You just can't say no. What would they think? Would they get mad at you? Would they think you were a jerk? If you told them no, would you feel like a jerk?

Take a minute and consider this scenario: Your mother/child/ spouse/sibling is seriously ill. You are getting ready to take him or her to the hospital when your coworker or friend calls. She just purchased a new cell phone, just like the one you have. She is on her way over so you can show her how to set up her voice mail. She can be there in five minutes.

How hard is it to say no in this instance? For most of us, it is not difficult at all. We experience no guilt, and we don't worry what she thinks. We know our priorities. We respectfully decline. We know how to say no when we are certain of our priorities. When dealing with a crisis (circumstantial dictatorship), saying no to other people's priorities is effortless.

How about this scenario: You have two hours blocked out of your extremely busy schedule to plan your life leadership activities and objectives for the next month and to review and update your vision statement. You are just sitting down at your desk when your coworker or friend calls. She just purchased a new cell phone, just like the one you have. She is on her way over so you can show her how set up her voice mail. She can be there in five minutes.

This time you are not in the middle of a crisis situation, but neither is your friend with the new cell phone. Can you say no as effortlessly as you did in the first scenario? You have to decide if your plan for your time is less important than your friend's plan for your time. Is the pursuit of your vision of success less important than your coworker's voicemail? If your answer is no, how do you tell her no without hurting her feelings or feeling like a jerk? I had to learn how to say no politely, respectfully, and free of guilt. Today I might say something like, "Susan, I would love to help you with your new phone, but I am booked up today with important projects. If you can stop by my house tomorrow after work, I will be glad to help you." In almost every instance, people either solve their own problems or find someone who is not "booked up" to help. Rarely do other people's priorities chase you into the next day.

One more scenario for you to consider: You have some free time this morning. You are thinking about maybe exercising or perhaps working on a business plan for a new idea you have. Your phone rings, and a friendly familiar voice on the other end says, "Hey buddy, what are you up to today?" **BEWARE! THIS IS A TRAP!** If you say, "Nothing," you can bet that other people's priorities are about to fill that void of "nothingness." When you acknowledge that you have nothing to do, saying no to other people's priorities is extremely difficult. If you don't have a plan for your life, someone else does! To own the life leadership position in your life, you must plan around your values, principles, and your Personal Vision of Success.

Helping other people is a big part of what makes me tick. I would never consider a career that did not offer me an opportunity to help other people. My values and principles require that I make myself available to my family and friends and that I am kind and helpful to all I encounter. I schedule time for these important activities, and I try to the best of my ability to incorporate these principles in all areas of my life. There are occasions in which other people are in a crisis (circumstantial dictatorships) that demands my immediate attention, and sometimes my agenda really isn't as important as that of the other person. We have to make these judgments based on our values and principles as to what our course of action should be. The more time you spend in life leadership, the clearer you will become as to what you value most, and consequently, you will intuitively know how to handle each situation as it arises.

Life Leadership and Circumstantial Dictatorships

Circumstantial dictatorships (crises) occur only in areas of great personal importance. There is no internal debate, no weighing of priorities; you spring into action as circumstances dictate. There is no need for time management once you find yourself here; just drop everything and deal with the crisis. If you are in true crisis mode, this is the highest and best use of your time. By focusing on areas of life leadership, it is possible to develop the same sense of certainty regarding the use of your time in nonemergency situations.

Wouldn't it be great to know ahead of time where the next circumstantial dictatorship is coming from? What if you could see a crisis coming far enough in advance that you could greatly reduce the impact it has on your life or maybe even prevent it from occurring altogether? Would you take preventive measures now if you knew what was coming? You already have in your possession a complete list of all of the areas in your life that a crisis could occur. It is your Personal Inventory of Values from Chapter 7. Crises occur only in the areas of our lives that we value most. For it to be a true circumstantial dictatorship, a situation in which circumstances dictate your next move, the crisis must hit close to home. If you read or hear about a fourteen-year-old child joining a street gang, it is a tragedy; discovering that your own fourteen-year-old child has joined a street gang is a crisis. Take a minute and consider your values. Can you think of a single circumstantial dictatorship (crisis) that could arise that isn't in an area of value?

Occasionally, lightning strikes, and there is no practical way to prevent it from happening. Most often, though, our crises are the direct result of neglected areas of life leadership. The important areas of our lives cannot be ignored forever. Either we choose to address our values, principles, and Personal Vision of Success through life leadership initiatives or we are forced to address them in circumstantial dictatorships.

If you are traveling by car on a desolate interstate highway, gasoline is of great value. If you regularly assess exactly where you stand regarding this "value," you have many options as to how you meet that need. Without any pressure or stress, you may choose an exit that offers easy re-entry to the highway, convenient restaurants, clean restrooms, the specific brand of gasoline you prefer, the best prices, and maybe even a mechanic on duty. Or you can wait until the "Low Fuel" light comes on and hope that you can make it to an exit with a gas station.

Life leadership is the regular assessment and alignment of our lives with our values, principles, and our Personal Visions of Success. The alternative to life leadership is an ever-expanding list of circumstantial dictatorships—midlife crises, divorce, chronic poor health, crisis of faith, estranged personal relationships, and bankruptcy, just to name a few. Investing in life leadership activities pays huge dividends in this area. The more time you spend in life leadership, the fewer circumstantial dictatorships you have to deal with, leaving you with even more time to invest in life leadership.

There is rarely ever any outside pressure to address areas of life leadership until they evolve into circumstantial dictatorships. Most discussions of values and principles are generic and superficial; specifics are intentionally avoided. It is not the responsibility of your friends and family to encourage you to define success, read for knowledge, exercise, eat healthy, work on your marriage, talk to your kids, seek spiritual enlightenment, or develop new relationships. The pressure to do so must come from within.

Life leadership does not suffer from the occasional random lightning strike so much as the known perils of neglected values and principles.

Life Leadership and Frivolous Diversions

Frivolous diversions are a double-edged sword. In moderation, they can be a source of great pleasure, an important aspect of a well-balanced life. Activities such as sailing, playing music, reading for pleasure, watching a good movie, relaxing on the beach, and taking weekend getaways with my wife are all, in my life plan, time well spent. Some of the juiciest parts of life are discovered through frivolous diversions, and because of this I am often tempted to linger a little too long in this area. As fallible human beings in pursuit of successes in life, we all have our crosses to bear. For me personally, there is no greater threat to my Personal Vision of Success than the unrestrained pursuit of frivolous diversions. It is my nature to skip dinner and go straight for the dessert. If a little is good, I say more would be better. I have learned, however, through firsthand experiences and by observing others, that pursuing frivolous diversions with reckless abandon will eventually lead my life from one crisis to the next, completely defeating my original purpose, which was simply to relax and have fun.

The American Heritage Dictionary defines diversion as "something that distracts the mind and relaxes or entertains." Who doesn't want this from time to time? It is only a problem when we are distracted to the point that we lose sight of our values and principles or we fail to focus our attention on the important task at hand.

I recently read a newspaper article about a woman who had to be rushed to the hospital to have a broken drill bit removed from her head. Her dentist, it was reported, liked the distraction of loud music as he drilled and filled cavities. This day, it seems he was so relaxed that he began carelessly dancing to the music as he drilled, breaking a drill bit off in the roof of the woman's mouth. He tried unsuccessfully to retrieve the broken bit, pushing it still further into the woman's head. It's a good thing he gave up when he did; the surgeon who successfully removed the drill bit informed the patient that her dentist was a fraction of an inch away from blinding her. What was the dentist thinking? He wasn't. He had intentionally distracted himself with a frivolous diversion.

With the exception of active alcoholics, drug addicts, and the mentally or emotionally unstable, most of us never suffer the complete melt-down in judgment that the dentist experienced regarding frivolous diversions. We don't skip our best friend's wedding to play a round of golf, we don't make ourselves late for work by watching reruns of *Gilligan's Island*, and we don't blow the rent money at the horse races. Our challenges are much more subtle. We sit down at our desk intending to work, only to spend the next three hours surfing the Internet. Instead of finishing our work, we wander down the hall looking for conversation, becoming someone else's "other," as in "other people's priorities." We come home from the office and plop down in front of the television until it is time to go to bed.

According to market information specialist the A. C. Nielsen Company, the average American watches more than four hours of TV each day[9], the equivalent of two months of nonstop television per year. Quite by accident, I discovered for myself just how much of my life I wasted in front of a television set. After the terrorist attacks on September 11, 2001, I became obsessed with watching television news. I was angry and frightened by the attacks, and I worried about the lasting effects they might have on our nation. I took every opportunity to park myself in front of a television. I had to know what was going on. I was so distracted by the media coverage of the search for Osama bin Laden that I was losing sleep, income, and peace of mind. Enough was enough! In November of 2001, I stopped watching television and reading the newspaper altogether. Suddenly, I had all this time on my hands, so I decided to spend it reading books on personal and professional development. I made huge gains in all of the important areas of my life, including my income and net worth. A year later, when I turned the TV back on, they were still looking for Osama bin Laden—I had not missed a thing! While most people can't imagine going a year without a newspaper or television, it enabled me to experience firsthand the benefits of investing time in life leadership.

An unexpected side effect of focusing on life leadership initiatives and gaining control over the important areas of my life is that I started getting the same buzz pursuing my Personal Vision of Success that I once sought through indulging in excessive frivolous diversions. The confidence and sense of accomplishment that is a natural by-product of working in areas of life leadership reduced my need for excessive frivolous diversions.

The next chapter is entirely devoted to the development of a simple tool that will easily enable you to focus on areas of life leadership as an exciting part of your day-to-day life.

CHAPTER

14

The Integrity Day Planner

Every competent boat captain I know has the most up-to-date nautical charts available when planning a voyage and refers to them often while underway. Even when day-sailing in well-known local waters, the use of all available navigational aids is the rule rather than the exception. To do anything less would endanger the vessel and those aboard unnecessarily. Chart books often include a quick reference section or an overview of the "rules of the road" because a well-placed channel marker is of little use if you are not sure whether you should leave it to port or starboard. Though there is much useful information to be found on nautical charts, they primarily serve two functions, the first of which is to enable the captain to plot a course prior to leaving port, which offers the ship safe passage to the desired destination. Second, by accurately locating and noting the ship's position on the chart while underway, the captain is able to quickly adjust the ship's heading as conditions require, maintaining steady progress along the intended course.

Wouldn't it be great if charts were available for your life, providing a way to plot the best course of action to reach your desired destination? Would your chart include the rules of the road to help you confidently choose the right direction at every confusing intersection? Considering that life conditions are ever changing, do you believe owning a tool that enables you to quickly assess and adjust the direction in which your life is heading would be beneficial? Would you like to be absolutely certain that you are making steady progress toward your Personal Vision of Success? The creation of just such a tool is exactly what we are going to do next, and the good news is that all of the heavy lifting is already done. In the previous chapters, you compiled all of the information needed to create your own personal Integrity Day Planner, a powerful tool that enables you to approach each day from the position of life leadership.

Let's set it up first, and then I will show you how to use it.

1. Go to www.premeditatedsuccess.com.

2. Click on the Download Book Tools icon.

3. Choose Download Integrity Day Planner Template.

4. Save the template to your computer.

Preview the example of the completed Integrity Day Planner on the following pages. On your computer, open your Integrity Day Planner template and complete the following steps:

•   Referring to Chapter 10: The Rules of Life, transfer your top five values and Rules to your Integrity Day Planner template.

- Referring to Chapter 11: A Front-End Alignment, transfer your prioritized Personal Vision of Success to the bottom right corner of your Integrity Day Planner.

- Please, go no further until you have completed steps 1 and 2.

- Complete the "Above all else" statement at the top of your Integrity Day Planner.

The "Above all else" statement should be short and sweet. Obviously, only one concept or dominant thought can truly be above all else. My "Above all else" statement has gotten progressively more concise over the years. Its most recent incarnation is "Above all else, enjoy life." This allows me to quickly assess how I am doing. If at any time I am not enjoying life, I know I need a change of direction in some area. Create an "Above all else" statement that will instantly tell you where you are. If you can't come up with one of your own, adopt mine. It's a great way to go through life!

When you are finished, save your personalized template as Integrity Day Planner-(DATE). You should now have the original blank template and your personalized Integrity Day Planner saved to your computer. I like to save my planners by date. It is interesting to look back and see how my priorities have evolved over time. Print out a copy or two of your personal Integrity Day Planner, and I will show you just how easy it is to begin mastering life leadership.

Above all else	
I enjoy the gift of _____ whenever	Day _____ Date ____/____/____
I enjoy the gift of _____ whenever	
I enjoy the gift of _____ whenever	**Professional Goals This Week**
	Personal Goals This Week
I enjoy the gift of _____ whenever	**I enjoy great success in life now that. . .**
	•
I enjoy the gift of _____ whenever	

Template Available at www.PreMeditatedSuccess.com

Above all else, enjoy life!

I enjoy the gift of Spiritual Growth whenever I pray or meditate, or I acknowledge the many gifts God has given me, or I attend any form of spiritual fellowship, or I read about spirituality, or my actions express gratitude, or I feel happy, healthy and prosperous, or I help others to grow spiritually.	**Day** ____Monday____ **Date**_11_/_19_/_08_

5:45	R. P. M.
9:00	Kristi - coaching
10:00	Pam - coaching
12:00	Lunch wit Bill
1:00	Write -
4:00	Workout
7:00	G :G

I enjoy the gift of Health and Fitness whenever I make healthy food choices, or I run for 10 or more minutes, or I walk on the beach, or I choose to take the stairs, or I lift weights, or I do 25 or more push-ups, or I do 25 or more crunches, or I park far away from the door, or I go surfing, or I go kayaking, or I go sailing, or I drink plenty of water, or I weigh between 168 and 176 lbs, or my energy fills the room.

I enjoy the gift of Family whenever I have fun with my family, or I am their #1 raving fan, or I am their sounding board, or I am contagiously enthusiastic, or I am the Dream Fulfillment Center, or I am Joyce's Sugar Daddy, or I am their best friend, or I am the wise and patient teacher, or I am the Magnificent Mood Dispenser, or I am their Rock of Support.

I enjoy the gift of Intelligence whenever I consider the long term implications of my decisions, or I seek experienced advice, or I read, or I pray and meditate, or I consider options at least 24 hours on important/non-urgent matters, or I attend personal development seminars, or I allow myself to be coached, or I teach others what I have learned.

I enjoy the gift of Wealth and Abundance whenever I focus on how easily and frequently money comes to me, or I speak of wealth and abundance, or I attract thoughts of financial independence, or I use my creative intelligence to create wealth, or I show others how to become wealthy, or I give generously to those in need.

Professional Goals This Week

Complete Chapter 14

16 new contracts

Personal Goals This Week

Lift weights X 2 Run X 2

Update Vision Board

I enjoy great success in life now that. . .

- I habitually seek spiritual knowledge and understanding
- I have the high-energy health and fitness of an athlete
- My relationship with my wife remains as passionate as the summer we met.
- My book is a National Bestseller
- I have taken 6 months off work to sail the Caribbean
- I encourage and assist my children as they pursue their visions of success
- Joyce and I are free to travel wherever we want, whenever we want.
- I am a deca-millionaire
- WRSC is first in market share
- I am a Nationally known speaker and writer

The Integrity Day Planner is intended to complement, not replace, your date book, calendar, Blackberry, Palm Pilot, or whatever tool you may be using for long-range planning and scheduling. The purpose here is not to see how many activities we can cram into a single day or to eliminate downtime through precise scheduling. It is about life leadership more so than time management.

The creation of the Integrity Day Planner came about through my efforts to increase the amount of time I was spending in the area life leadership. The purpose of this tool is to align my life with my values, principles, and my Personal Vision of Success to the best of my ability. I know it sounds like a lot of work, but I found it to be an amazingly simple thing to do.

You will notice right away that the Integrity Day Planner is different from most time management systems. About 75 percent of the page is dedicated to your values and your Personal Vision of Success. Although both of these should be reviewed and updated periodically, they do not change from day to day; therefore, we have "hard-wired" them into your planning tool. Your top five values and your new rules for meeting those values take up the left half of your planner, and the bottom right corner is reserved for your Personal Vision of Success. Immediately above your Personal Vision of Success is a space for you to identify two personal goals and two professional goals to be accomplished this week. Before we go any further, let's examine the difference between a goal and a vision.

A goal and a vision are not the same thing. A goal is the purpose toward which an endeavor is directed. A vision is a vivid, imaginative conception or anticipation of that which will come to be. I have found that some people (whom I call goalies) are goal-driven, enjoying the structure and accountability associated with goal setting, while others like me are vision-driven; we don't overly concern ourselves with details and timelines. I have benefited greatly by incorporating structured goals into my life leadership, and I have witnessed amazing results among the goalies who have allowed themselves the luxury of dreaming without constraints. Both vision and goals play important roles in life leadership.

Notice on page 143 under my Personal Vision of Success the statement, "I enjoy great success in life now that I have the high-energy health and fitness of an athlete." This is what I anticipate coming to be. Notice how consistent this vision statement is with the value of health and fitness. Now look under the heading of Personal Goals This Week. I have "lift weights x 2 run x 2," meaning my goal for this week is to lift weights twice and go running twice. The last couple of weeks I have not been as consistent with my exercise as I like, so this week I set this goal for myself as a minimum.

Wouldn't I get the same results by just taking action on the goal without fooling around with visions or values? I have tried that approach many times in the past without success. My problem is that when I look down at a piece of paper that just says "run two times a week and lift weights two times a week," it doesn't always look like fun. In fact, sometimes it looks and feels like punishment. It is just too easy for me to blow off those things that feel like punishment. When I read my Personal Vision of Success and see "I enjoy great success in life now that I have the high-energy health and fitness of an athlete," I am inspired. In my mind's eye, I not only picture myself as an athlete, I feel like an athlete. Athletes are passionate about running and lifting weights. It is easy for me to achieve my goal of running and lifting weights this week. My vision is my thoughts, my attitude, and my expectations; my goals are my appropriate actions and predictable results. Visions and goals are important components in the PreMeditated Model of Success.

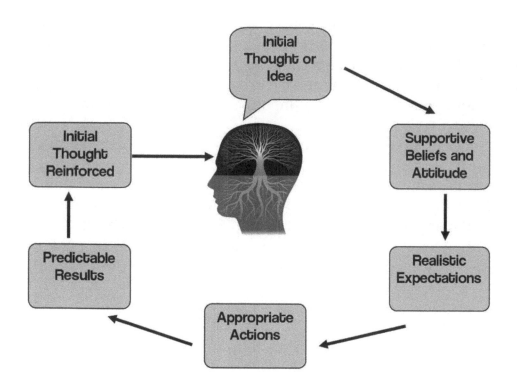

One of the most popular methods of setting goals today is the S.M.A.R.T. method. To be considered S.M.A.R.T., your goals must be Specific, Measurable, Achievable, Realistic, and Time-bound. I understand the reasoning behind this method. It is accountability. Without accountability, what many people refer to as goals are really nothing more than an ambiguous wish list, lacking clarity and commitment. S.M.A.R.T. goals are great for moving you forward through relatively short increments of time. However, if you attempt to use this method for long-range planning, it will suck the life right out of your dreams.

I have attended goal-writing workshops in which participants were led through the process of writing one-year goals, two- to three-year goals, five-year goals, ten-year goals, and twenty-year goals. We would begin by writing nonstop for ten minutes, listing everything we wanted to have, accomplish, or become in life, and then specifying the appropriate time frame in which these goals would be accomplished; one year, two to three years, five years, or ten to twenty years. I could easily apply the S.M.A.R.T. method to my one-year goals. Seeing these goals on paper motivated and energized me. I was so certain these things would be mine that I couldn't wait to get started.

When I looked at my long-range goals, however, especially those that were five or more years away, the S.M.A.R.T. method had the opposite effect, draining my energy and enthusiasm. How specific can I be about a goal that may be ten years down the road? Why would I intend for it to take that long anyway? Why would I want my view of the future to be limited by what is achievable and realistic by today's standard? I could either dumb down my long-term goals to make them S.M.A.R.T., or I could approach them as an exciting vision of my future. I chose the latter.

The Integrity Day Planner encourages you to incubate your dreams without allowing them to die of neglect. Each week we set four goals, two personal and two professional. It is not enough for these foals to be S.M.A.R.T. They must be S.M.A.R.T.eR: Specific, **M**easurable, **A**chievable, **R**ealistic, **T**ime-bound, and **R**elevant. By "relevant," I mean relevant to your Personal Vision of Success and your system of values.

Again, let's refer to the example on page 143. The first professional goal I have for this week is "Complete Chapter 14." That is what I am working on right now. This goal is relevant to my Personal Vision of Success because it specifies that I want my book to be a national best seller and to become a nationally known speaker and writer. This goal also meets four of my top five values by teaching others and passing on knowledge. The goal of securing sixteen new contracts this week is relevant to my vision of WRSC (my real estate company) becoming number one in market share. It puts me a few steps closer to decamillionaire status and being free to travel as I please. My ability to assist my children and to take six months off work to sail the Caribbean are both improved by this goal, and obviously it is relevant to my value of wealth and abundance. We have already discussed how my personal goal for exercising is tied to my values and vision of success.

At first it may feel as if you are setting the bar too low by focusing on goals that can be accomplished in just a week's time, but you will soon discover that you are moving forward at an amazing pace. Over the course of a single year, you will take action on over two hundred S.M.A.R.T.eR. goals, propelling you forward in the pursuit of your Personal Vision of Success.

At the beginning of each week, open your Integrity Day Planner on your computer, type in your S.M.A.R.T.eR. goals, and print out the five or seven planners that you will need for the coming week. Whether you prefer to plan the night before or the morning of, plan only one day at a time! Schedule weekly and monthly; plan daily. Let's look at the planning portion of the Integrity Day Planner, located in the top right corner just below the Day and Date line. You have room for eleven appointments or activities. The "time" box is intentionally left blank. I normally get up between 5:00 and 6:00 AM, and I may have commitments as late as 9:00 PM.

A typical day planner page covering 8:00 AM to 6:00 PM in fifteen-minute increments doesn't accurately cover my life or the lives of most people I know. The "blank box" approach enables you to plan in a way that matches your life rather than trying to schedule your life to match your planner. You may have noticed "R.P.M." on the first line of my planner; it is short for "read, pray, and mediate." This is a personal daily commitment I have made to read for personal development and to seek spiritual growth through prayer and meditation. I have this "hardwired" into my planner, and it is the very first thing I do each day.

After my R.P.M. time, I date my planner and read through my values and my Personal Vision of Success. I then refer to my date book for any appointments that I have scheduled for the day. On the example on page 143, I have three appointments in my date book: two coaching sessions, one at 9:00 AM and one at 10:00 AM, and a community service commitment at 7:00 PM. I write these appointments onto my Integrity Day Planner. I review my goals for the week and schedule goal-related activities to the extent that my schedule permits. On the day of my example, I was able to schedule time to work on my book and exercise. I also thought it would be nice to have lunch with a friend of mine if his schedule permitted (it didn't work out, but I made the effort). Each day, I read through my values and vision statement, looking for ways to incorporate these into the everyday aspects of my life. I am ready for the day! Excluding my commitment to R.P.M., my entire day is planned in a matter of minutes, and I know I am one day closer to my Personal Vision of Success. I stick my Integrity Day Planner into my date book, referring to it throughout the day. I am reminded to "enjoy life" and to focus my attention on the things that matter most.

You may have a job or other commitment that requires you to keep specific hours doing specific tasks. It may feel as if you don't have control over your own life during that time. Applying your values and principles to all of your affairs gives you control of your life at all times. How can you be a positive influence in the lives of others? How can you meet your own objectives as you meet the objectives of your employer? What discretionary time can you devote to this week's goals?

I like to get up in the morning before anyone else in the house. This is when I read, pray, meditate, and plan my day. I have come to really value this quiet time to myself. I suggest you carve out a chunk of time that is entirely devoted to life leadership planning as well. It doesn't have to be at 5:00 AM; that is just what works for me. You might find the same thing at midnight that I found in the morning. Even if it is just a few minutes every day, the effect it will have on your life will amaze you.

I encourage you to print out your Integrity Day Planner and use a pen or pencil to physically write in your appointments and activities. This may be hard for some of the more technology-driven readers, but it really is worth the trouble. Putting a pen to paper is a stronger commitment. Most people have difficulty misleading themselves in their own handwriting. Having your Personal Vision of Success, along with your top five values and your goals for the week, in your hands on 8-1/2 x 11 paper does something to you that scrolling down a computer screen just can't do. I can't explain why it is different; it just is. Try it for yourself, and I think you will agree. Throughout the day, refer to your Integrity Day Planner whenever you have some downtime or are simply checking to see what you have to do next. If you are troubled or irritated, often you will find that your actions are not consistent with your values or that an element of your Personal Vision of Success is suffering from neglect. If your job requires you to create a to-do list in order to keep up with a high volume of tasks that can be accomplished in a short period of time, make your to-do list on the back of your Integrity Day Planner. The idea here is to make life leadership issues press against you in the same manner that other people's priorities press against you. I have found that my Integrity Day Planner is a powerful tool in warding off other people's priorities. When I pull out my planner that is filled with important activities, it is so easy to say no. I believe once you assume the position of life leadership, you will not choose to return to a position of subordination.

For those of you who are committed to scheduling on a PDA and still want the benefits of Integrity Based Planning, you will find the Integrity Weekly Planner under the Download Book Tools section of PreMeditatedSuccess.com. After downloading the file, set it up just like the Integrity Day Planner. This tool will enable you to review your top five values and your Personal Vision of Success as you set your weekly goals while relying on your PDA to schedule specific activities. If you go this route, be sure to schedule time every week to set values and vision-based goals for yourself. Make time to schedule and plan your very first life leadership activity.

CHAPTER

15

Vivid Anticipation

I love to plan vacations far in advance. I do so not because I fear overlooking some important detail or out of worry that my favorite resort will sell out; I do so because I start getting excited about my vacation the minute I commit to it. Whenever I stumble across the dates on my calendar, I imagine the warm Caribbean sun on my back, my wife in a bathing suit so small she will only wear it in foreign countries, no cell phones, no meetings, no deadlines. In the middle of a hectic day, I find myself in full-blown vacation mode. What a great gift I have given myself. I get to enjoy my vacation from the moment the idea is born. This positive state of vivid anticipation is *almost* as good as the actual vacation.

Vivid anticipation is the extreme sports version of "as a man thinketh." It is the difference between a thought and a vision; it is the energy that fuels the law of attraction. Have you ever experienced the positive effects of vivid anticipation similar to those I described in the previous paragraph when you just knew that great things were coming your way, like a child the night before Christmas? Ah, life is good, isn't it? How about the negative effects of vivid anticipation? Have you ever anticipated really bad news? Have you ever vividly anticipated getting dumped, being fired, falling ill, going broke, screwing up, forgetting your lines, singing off key, being made fun of, or blowing your big chance? Ah, life stinks, doesn't it?

When we vividly anticipate good stuff, life is great. When we vividly anticipate bad stuff, life is torturous. Personally, I prefer great over torturous. A few years ago, I was introduced to a vivid anticipation tool that breathed life into my Personal Vision of Success. That tool is the vision board.

When we think, we think in pictures and images, not in written words. When I think about wealth and abundance, I don't think about a bunch of wrinkled-up dollar bills or a bank statement with a bunch of zeros. I see a beautiful creek- front vacation home on Bald Head Island; I picture myself sailing on my brand new Island Packet 485; I imagine buying my son Will an original 1958 Gibson Les Paul guitar or handing my son David the keys to a new car. I don't picture the money—I picture how much fun I will have spending it! When I think of traveling, I don't picture myself sitting on a plane. I see crystal clear water and white sandy beaches; I see hammocks and sunsets. The purpose of a vision board is to bring those images to life, and if you will allow yourself to be a kid again, it's a whole lot of fun.

To create a vision board, you will need the same supplies that got you through kindergarten: school glue, scissors, poster board, and a stack of magazines. A vision board is a collage of images and pictures that passionately represent your Personal Vision of Success. Because we are dealing with topics that you are already passionate about, there is a very good chance you have all of the images and pictures you need to complete this project lying around your house. If you come up short, head to a bookstore or any place with a great selection of magazines and find the images that inspire vivid anticipation.

My vision boards have included pictures of exotic islands, sailboats in the tropical seas, oceanfront houses, million dollar bills, things that I will own, and things I will buy for others. They include a best-sellers list that I created with my book in the number one position, a firm ranking report with my real estate company on top, inspirational quotes, and reminders. The only rule I have is that it must generate a feeling of vivid anticipation. If I ever find myself in a funk for a few days, one of the best ways I know of to get out of it is to add new images to my vision board and spend time looking at it several times a day. It is amazing how quickly my positive outlook on life returns.

One winter day, I wrote a $400,000 check to myself, dated it March 29, and stuck it up on my vision board. When I wrote the check, I was working on a deal to raise capital for one of my businesses, and I had a pretty good idea where the money was coming from. Shortly after writing the check, however, the deal fell apart, but I never got around to taking the check off of my board. Months later, just as I was preparing to leave town on vacation, a deal quickly came together with another investor who promptly mailed me a check in the amount of $400,000, dated March 29. I could almost hear the theme music from *The Twilight Zone* when I realized what had happened. That particular vision board was very productive. My sailboat (the exact model) and the book you are now reading both began as images on my vision board. Is it just coincidence? You believe what you choose to believe. As for what I believe, all I can tell you is that the check on my vision board right now is made out for a lot more than $400,000!

CHAPTER

16

The Law of Projected Energy

W hen I was fourteen years old, I went camping on Shackleford Banks off the coast of North Carolina. The only source of fresh water on the island was a well and an old-fashioned hand pump. In order to draw water from the well, you first had to prime the pump by pouring a little bit of water back into the well through the pump. I am not sure why it worked that way; all I know is that if you didn't prime the pump, you didn't get any water. To get some, I had to give some.

The law of projected energy works much the same way. I view the law of projected energy as the proactive cousin of the law of attraction—not only visualizing the harvest but planting seeds as well.

Planting seeds to meet our needs is exactly what the law of projected energy is all about. Whenever I am discouraged, I have found that the quickest and best way to overcome it is by encouraging others. One of my most glaring shortcomings is my lack of patience. This is especially true when I have to wait in line or when I get caught in heavy traffic. I have discovered that I can prime the pump with patience by acting on opportunities to let other people or cars go ahead of me. The traffic may not lighten up, the line may not move any faster, but my frustration and impatience disappear.

Whether your need is love, tolerance, understanding, patience, kindness, financial assistance, or just about anything else you can think of, somewhere out there another person is trying to attract that very same thing into their lives. Perhaps our perceived need is really just a calling for us to answer that need in someone else's life. When our eyes are open, the opportunities to plant seeds are all around us.

A Pleasant Surprise

Isn't it nice when someone pays you a sincere, unexpected compliment, a sincere, relevant acknowledgement of some form of greatness that you are exhibiting? To be on the receiving end of such a heartfelt compliment is always a pleasant surprise, instantly lightening your load. Wouldn't it be great if every time you really needed an energetic shot in the arm, there was a sincere compliment awaiting you?

You know what I have discovered? There is always a sincere compliment awaiting me; mostly though, they are "awaiting me" to deliver them, not receive them. And you know what else I've discovered? This is another way that it is much better to give than to receive—better in that I can enjoy the benefits as often as I choose and better in that my attention is on the greatness of others and away from my own struggles.

Whenever I endeavor to lift the spirits of another person, I find my own spirit lifted as well. If you really want to make a difference in a person's life, there is a sincere compliment awaiting your delivery. Be a pleasant surprise!

Gifts for the Greater Good

Each of us possesses a gift, a talent, a life experience, or an area of expertise that uniquely qualifies us to serve the greater good in some capacity. With very few exceptions, the remarkably successful among us share a strong desire to help others, to give back in a meaningful way. Nonprofit foundations established by Tiger Woods, Oprah Winfrey, Anthony Robbins, and others like them impact the lives of millions of people through charitable contributions, youth mentoring programs, charter schools, prison outreach programs, programs to aid the homeless, meal distribution organizations, and many other strategic initiatives created for the sole purpose of improving the lives of other people. It's not just the celebrities' fame that lends credibility to their respective foundations; it is their character. We trust them to do the right thing with our donations.

The opportunities to serve others are endless. Eric Clapton, a recovering addict and alcoholic, founded Crossroads Centre, an addiction treatment facility located on the island of Antigua. In a letter that Clapton posted on the center's website, he stated, "My vision was to create a Centre of the highest caliber to treat people of the Caribbean and throughout the world. The Centre would be staffed with experienced and internationally recognized professionals. The cost of treatment would be held to the lowest possible level, ensuring affordability and accessibility. And most importantly, this non-profit Centre would provide treatment scholarships for people of the Caribbean region and around the world.".

Sometimes our greatest gifts are forged through times of great adversity, and it is this life experience that we have to offer for the greater good. Some of the most effective counselors in the field of alcohol and drug abuse are recovering alcoholics and drug addicts. It is the survivors of domestic violence, sexual abuse, cancer, violent crime, and other extreme situations who are most qualified to assist others through the same challenges.

Perhaps you have some specialized knowledge that you can share with others; maybe you can mentor a young person through the start-up of a business. Is there someone you can coach? Is there a workshop you can facilitate? Can you teach someone to read?

I believe reading is the most important skill a person can possess. Mastering this skill enables a person to master many other skills. I will shamelessly take this opportunity to promote First Book[10], my favorite nonprofit organization. First Book puts books in the hands of underprivileged children free of charge. The excitement on their faces when they realize they can take these books home, that they are theirs to keep, is something to witness. Teaching children to read is a critical step in overcoming generational poverty, and if you are looking for a way to make a difference, consider contributing to your local chapter of First Book. If by some chance there is not a chapter in your area, start one!

So, can we, the anonymous masses, really serve the greater good in a meaningful way? Absolutely. In fact, we can serve in ways that the recognizably famous cannot. If I was going though a soup line and Tiger Woods or Anthony Robbins were dipping up the soup, I would have to at least try to strike up a conversation, slowing down the line and prolonging the hunger of all those behind me.

Whenever we give, we receive even more in return, but that is not the primary reason we give. We give and we help because we can. It is not the contribution we can't make that causes unnecessary suffering; it's the contribution we *don't* make. For anyone who wants to contribute a gift for the greater good, there is a welcoming place for you to serve, a void in which only you are uniquely qualified to fill.

Student Teacher

According to the PreMeditated Model of Success, what is the very first thing you must address in order to create lasting change in your life? The answer, of course, is your thinking. Everything else follows. If you are going to change your reality, you first must change your thinking. Old ideas and old thoughts are incapable of producing new results. We need new ideas and a deeper level of thinking if we want tomorrow to be different than today. So how do we get our same old brain to kick out some new material on a regular basis? Only a continuous stream of education can produce a continuous stream of new thoughts and ideas. It is a daily commitment to learning, a student-for-life approach to education, that will keep you moving forward.

If you have completed your education, you are fully prepared for the way things used to be. You see, the world is ever changing, and it is impossible to stay in one place. You are either moving forward or moving backward; you are either expanding your mental capacities or getting progressively "dumber" in relation to the rest of the world. Do you remember when Windows 95 was the best, most up-to-date operating system you could have on your computer? When Windows 95 was introduced, all of the earlier versions became obsolete. You absolutely had to have it to run the most popular software programs. When was the last time you saw someone using Windows 95? How long does it take to go from latest and greatest to functionally obsolete? It can happen so fast that your head will spin! Everything else is moving forward. If you choose to stand still, you are choosing to fall behind. I am not saying that a daily commitment to learning will get you ahead of the pack; I am saying you need this *just to keep up* with the pack.

Your personal commitment to learning is a function of life leadership. It is unlikely that anyone will pressure you to continue your education; it has to come from within. This is an area of life in which the proper use of discipline pays huge dividends. If you will commit to being a student for life, you can have and become whatever you can imagine.

To start, simply *decide* to start. Schedule a chunk of time every day to continue your education. I like to read, but that is just one of many options. You may prefer audio books or podcasts. There are some excellent personal development programs available on CD and DVD. I began by making a few simple changes in my routine. Instead of reading the local newspaper first thing in the morning, I began reading books for personal development; instead of listening to the radio in my car, I began listening to audio books or seminars on CD. It really isn't difficult.

Becoming a student for life enables you to keep pace with the rest of the world; becoming a *teacher* for life moves you ahead of the pack. It is by teaching that the student owns the lesson. As you gain knowledge, ideas, and inspiration, pass them on to anyone who will have them. The opportunities to teach are all around you, in your home, your work, your team, your church, and your neighborhood.

As you learn new ideas and concepts, think about how you might teach them to another person and you will learn at a much deeper level. When the teacher is ready, the student will appear. We plant the seed of learning best by teaching, and a student teacher is a powerful gift for the greater good.

Seeds of Faith

PreMeditated Success is a program built upon spiritual concepts. The lessons contained in this book, from values and integrity to taking action based on beliefs and serving the greater good, are spiritual principles—concepts that have been taught for centuries by history's greatest teachers and spiritual leaders. Great books on personal development and success have been around for hundreds of years. Although the presentation and primary areas of emphasis often appear to be unique, the underlying message of these books is amazingly consistent. Though our voices are different, the song itself remains the same. Let's examine the spiritual nature of the PreMeditated Model of Success.

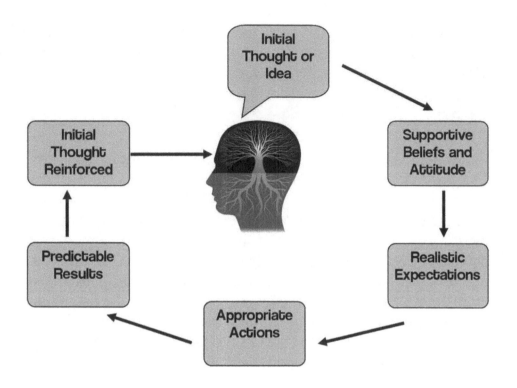

Mediation is a spiritual term defined as "continued or extended thought; reflection; contemplation"—the first step in the PreMeditated Model of Success. From this meditative state, our beliefs develop. Our belief system shapes our attitude, and expectations are formed. Belief is the seed of faith. It is by taking action on our beliefs, and experiencing the results of those actions, that faith is born and our meditations are reinforced. The circle is unbroken.

Human beings are spiritual beings. Personal growth is spiritual growth. All lasting change, for better or for worse, is the direct result of spiritual growth or spiritual neglect. We can expand what we are and become less of what we are, but we cannot become other than what we are. We are spiritual beings. It took me a very long time to understand that. In my personal experience, spiritual growth has come about by examining my thoughts and beliefs through daily prayer and meditation, by acting in a manner that is consistent with my beliefs to the *best of my ability*, thus expanding my faith as the result of my actions and validating my beliefs. Whenever I scrimp on prayer and meditation or I carelessly and consistently act in a manner that is in conflict with my beliefs, my faith begins to waver and my spirit begins to shrink. I am either progressing, or I am regressing. I have found it impossible to merely maintain a level of spirituality.

It is not my purpose here to tell you what to believe but to encourage you instead to think about what you believe, to examine your beliefs in the light of prayer and/or meditation, to seek clarity, and to *know* that the path you have chosen is the right path for you. As you identify your beliefs more precisely, acting upon them will become second nature. It is in this manner that the seed of belief grows into working faith. Faith is powerful stuff. With it I am fearless in the face of storms; without it no harbor feels safe. Success is unimaginable to me in the absence of faith.

CHAPTER

17

Playful Pursuit

I like to fish. Sometimes I'll make a meal of my catch, but mostly I just let them go. I don't know what the exact ratio is, but considering all of the time I have spent fishing in my life, I'm guessing that for every minute that I actually had a fish on the line, I probably have two or three hours of time with no evidence at all that fish even exist. There have been plenty of fishless fishing trips in my past. You know what the funny thing is about fishing? I enjoy the fishless trips just as much as those during which the fish are biting. It is the act of fishing that I enjoy, *even more* than catching fish! This may sound stupid, but I know it is true for me. If I caught a fish on every single cast, without exception, no matter what bait I was using, in any weather, at any time, I would quickly lose all interest in fishing. Yet I can spend days on end without a bite and maintain my enthusiasm. Yes, it is the act of fishing that I enjoy. I spend my day convinced that I am going to catch a state record something-or-other on the very next cast. How could I possibly get bored or discouraged when I know that this cast will produce a state record?

I am happiest when I apply this "next cast" mentality to all areas of my life. I believe the playful pursuit of success is success! Think about it: for every minute of time you spend realizing your dreams, how many days, months, or even years, are spent in pursuit of those dreams? Isn't the playful pursuit of your dreams at least as valuable as the dreams themselves? What would you do if every single one of your dreams were suddenly realized? What if you caught *all* the fish? Be grateful that some of the "big ones" get away, leaving us something to pursue tomorrow. Enjoy the fishing!

FREE BONUS AUDIO

The Discipline Myth Exposed

Visit www.PreMeditatedSuccess.com for your FREE BONUS download.

Would you like to pass PreMeditated Success along to someone you care about?

The audio version of *PreMeditated Success in Life* is available on compact disc. To order, please visit our website, www.PreMeditatedSuccess.com, where you will also find:

- Live events, seminars, and workshops

- LifeSuccess coaching

- Business consultation

- E-books

- Free downloads

- PreMeditated Success message board

- PreMeditated Success information blog

At PreMeditated Success, our seminars, workshops, personal results coaching programs, and corporate staff development plans are tailored to meet your specific vision and purpose. Whether you are an individual seeking personal wealth and achievement or a company ready to exponentially increase sales and profitability, it is our job not only to inspire but to guide you through the process of setting and achieving meaningful, strategically defined goals.

PreMeditated Success
1011 Highway 17 South, North Myrtle Beach, S.C. 29582
scott@premeditatedsuccess.com
Office: 843-663-0080 • Fax: 843-280-8884
www.PreMeditatedSuccess.com

REFERENCES

1   Dictionary.com

2   Dictionary.com

3   World Institute for Development Economics Research of the United Nations University, December 5, 2006.

4   Bill & Melinda Gates Foundation. http://www.gatesfoundation.org (accessed October 2007).

5   Myers Barnes Associates, Inc. http://www.myersbarnes.com (accessed October 2007).

6   Visit www.thesecret.tv for more information on The Secret.

7   The American Heritage Dictionary of the English Language, Fourth Edition, 2006.

8   Jessica Long.org. www.jessicalong.org (accessed December 2007).

9   Compiled by TV-Free America, http://www.csun.edu/science/health/docs/tv&health.html (accessed November 2007).

10 First Book. www.firstbook.org.

ABOUT THE AUTHOR

Scott Jackson makes his home in North Myrtle Beach, South Carolina, with his wife Joyce and sons David and Will.

A successful business owner, author, master sales trainer, and LifeSuccess consultant, Scott has personally mentored, coached, and assisted hundreds of clients and associates in the pursuit of their Personal Visions of Success.

9 781600 375187